Implementing the NIST
Cybersecurity Framework

CYBERSECURITY NEXUS

ISACA®
Trust in, and value from, information systems

www.isaca.org/cyber

About ISACA®

With more than 115,000 constituents in 180 countries, ISACA (*www.isaca.org*) helps business and IT leaders build trust in, and value from, information and information systems. Established in 1969, ISACA is the trusted source of knowledge, standards, networking, and career development for information systems audit, assurance, security, risk, privacy and governance professionals. ISACA offers the Cybersecurity Nexus™, a comprehensive set of resources for cybersecurity professionals, and COBIT®, a business framework that helps enterprises govern and manage their information and technology. ISACA also advances and validates business-critical skills and knowledge through the globally respected Certified Information Systems Auditor® (CISA®), Certified Information Security Manager® (CISM®), Certified in the Governance of Enterprise IT® (CGEIT®) and Certified in Risk and Information Systems Control™ (CRISC™) credentials. The association has more than 200 chapters worldwide.

Disclaimer

ISACA has designed and created *Implementing the NIST Cybersecurity Framework* ("the Work") primarily as an educational resource for assurance, governance, risk and security professionals. ISACA makes no claim that use of any of the Work will assure a successful outcome. The Work should not be considered inclusive of all proper information, procedures and tests or exclusive of other information, procedures and tests that are reasonably directed to obtaining the same results. In determining the propriety of any specific information, procedure or test, assurance, governance, risk and security professionals should apply their own professional judgment to the specific circumstances presented by the particular systems or information technology environment.

Reservation of Rights

ISACA

3701 Algonquin Road, Suite 1010
Rolling Meadows, IL 60008 USA
Phone: +1.847.253.1545
Fax: +1.847.253.1443
Email: *info@isaca.org*
Web site: *www.isaca.org*

Provide feedback: *www.isaca.org/US-cyber-implementation*
Participate in the ISACA Knowledge Center: *www.isaca.org/knowledge-center*
Follow ISACA on Twitter: *https://twitter.com/ISACANews*
Join ISACA on LinkedIn: ISACA (Official), *http://linkd.in/ISACAOfficial*
Like ISACA on Facebook: *www.facebook.com/ISACAHQ*

Implementing the NIST Cybersecurity Framework
ISBN 978-1-60420-357-8

Acknowledgments

Development Team
Greg Witte, CISM, CISSP-ISSEP, PMP, G2 Inc., USA
Tom Conkle, CISSP, G2 Inc., USA

Workshop Participants
Louis Aponte, ITIL, Weber State University, USA
Raymond R. Czech, CISSP, Las Vegas Sands Corp., USA
Christopher J. Egan, CISA, CRISC, IBM, USA
Meenu Gupta, CISA, CISM, CBP, CIPP, CISSP, PMP, Mittal Technologies, USA
Carlo Morgano, CISA, CGEIT, CRISC, EQT Corporation, USA
Tim Virtuc, Texas.Gov, USA
Ernest W. Wohnig III, CISM, PMP, System 1 Inc., USA

Expert Reviewers
Jim W. Gearhart, CISA, CGEIT, CRISC, Federal Reserve Bank of Richmond, USA
Norman Kromberg, CISA, CGEIT, CRISC, CQA, NBE, ACI Worldwide, USA
Theodore Lloyd, CISM, NTT Com Security, USA
Jeff Lukins, CISA, CISSP, CIPP/IT, CEH, MCSE, MSE, Dynetics, USA
Vincent Orrico, Ph.D., CISA, CGEIT, CRISC, CBCLA, CBCP, C|CISO, CISSP, PMP,
    Teachers College, Columbia University, USA
T.J. Short, Global Cash Access, USA

ISACA Board of Directors
Robert E Stroud, CGEIT, CRISC, CA, USA, International President
Steven A. Babb, CGEIT, CRISC, ITIL, Vodafone, UK, Vice President
Garry J. Barnes, CISA, CISM, CGEIT, CRISC, BAE Systems Detica, Australia, Vice President
Robert A. Clyde, CISM, Adaptive Computing, USA, Vice President
Ramses Gallego, CISM, CGEIT, CCSK, CISSP, SCPM, Six Sigma Black Belt, Dell, Spain,
    Vice President
Theresa Grafenstine, CISA, CGEIT, CRISC, CGAP, CGMA, CIA, CPA, US House of Representatives,
    USA, Vice President
Vittal R. Raj, CISA, CISM, CGEIT, CRISC, CFE, CIA, CISSP, FCA, Kumar & Raj, India,
    Vice President
Tony Hayes, CGEIT, AFCHSE, CHE, FACS, FCPA, FIIA, Queensland Government, Australia, Past
    International President
Gregory T. Grocholski, CISA, The Dow Chemical Co., USA, Past International President
Debbie A. Lew, CISA, CRISC, Ernst & Young LLP, USA, Director
Frank K.M. Yam, CISA, CIA, FHKCS, FHKIoD, Focus Strategic Group Inc., Hong Kong, Director
Alexander Zapata Lenis, CISA, CGEIT, CRISC, ITIL, PMP, Grupo Cynthus S.A. de C.V.,
    Mexico, Director

Knowledge Board
Steven A. Babb, CGEIT, CRISC, ITIL, Vodafone, UK, Chairman
Rosemary M. Amato, CISA, CMA, CPA, Deloitte Touche Tohmatsu Ltd., The Netherlands
Neil Patrick Barlow, CISA, CISM, CRISC, CISSP, IntercontinentalExchange, Inc. NYSE, UK
Charlie Blanchard, CISA, CISM, CRISC, ACA, CIPP/E, CIPP/US, CISSP, FBCS, Amgen Inc., USA
Sushil Chatterji, CGEIT, Edutech Enterprises, Singapore
Phil J. Lageschulte, CGEIT, CPA, KPMG LLP, USA
Anthony P. Noble, CISA, Viacom, USA
Jamie Pasfield, CGEIT, ITIL V3, MSP, PRINCE2, Pfizer, UK
Ivan Sanchez Lopez, CISA, CISM, CISSP, ISO 27001 LA, DHL Global Forwarding & Freight, Germany

Acknowledgments *(cont.)*

Cybersecurity Task Force
Eddie Schwartz, CISA, CISM, CISSP, MCSE, PMP, USA, Chairman
Manuel Aceves, CISA, CISM, CGEIT, CRISC, CISSP, FCITSM, Cerberian Consulting,
    SA de CV, Mexico
Sanjay Bahl, CISM, CIPP, India
Neil Patrick Barlow, CISA, CISM, CRISC, CISSP, IntercontinentalExchange, Inc. NYSE, UK
Brent Conran, CISA, CISM, CISSP, USA
Derek Grocke, HAMBS, Australia
Samuel Linares, CISA, CISM, CGEIT, CRISC, CISSP, GICSP, Industrial Cybersecurity
    Center (CCI), Spain
Marc Sachs, Verizon, USA

Contents

List of Figures

Page intentionally left blank

Executive Summary

Information is a key resource for all organizations. The operational technology (OT) and information technology (IT) that support information are increasingly advanced, pervasive and connected. They are also under increasing attack. Destructive assaults against financial, retail and energy providers indicate a need for renewed dedication to management of technology-related risk at an acceptable level. Many organizations recognize this challenge, but need help charting a road map to protect valuable business assets. They need an approach that draws on the success of others through manageable processes and measurable improvement. This document describes proven practices to exploit opportunity through a better understanding of organizational risk and active management processes. This guide enables the reader to implement ISACA methods as an effective way to use the Cybersecurity Framework (described in the following paragraph). Application of these components enables communication about priorities and activities in business terms, turning potential organizational risk into competitive advantage.

In 2013, US President Obama issued Executive Order (EO) 13636, *Improving Critical Infrastructure Cybersecurity*. The EO called for the development of a voluntary risk-based cybersecurity framework (the Cybersecurity Framework, or CSF) that is "prioritized, flexible, repeatable, performance-based, and cost-effective." The CSF was developed through an international partnership of small and large organizations, including owners and operators of the nation's critical infrastructure, with leadership by the National Institute of Standards and Technology (NIST). The CSF provides a risk-based approach that enables rapid success and steps to increasingly improve cybersecurity maturity. Because these values closely mirror the governance and management principles that ISACA has fostered for many years, ISACA practices were a natural fit as an implementation road map. ISACA participated in the CSF's development and helped embed key principles from the COBIT framework into the industry-led effort. Because of this harmony, implementation of the CSF using ISACA processes is seamless and enables the results promised by the Cybersecurity Framework while leveraging the lessons learned over fifty years of ISACA success.

This guide maps to each of the CSF steps and activities, extending the CSF guidance with practical and measurable activities. Achieving CSF objectives using ISACA methods helps to leverage operational risk understanding in a business context, enabling the organization to be proactive and competitive. This approach, in turn, enables proactive value to the organization's stakeholders, translating high-level enterprise goals into manageable, specific goals rather than a disconnected checklist model.

While the CSF was originally intended to support critical infrastructure providers, it is applicable to any organization that wishes to better manage and reduce cybersecurity risk. Nearly all organizations, in some way, are part of critical infrastructure. Each is connected to critical functions as a consumer through the global economy, through telecommunication services and in many other ways. Improved risk management by each member of this ecosystem will, ultimately, reduce cybersecurity risk globally.

As key participants in the CSF development, including an active role in national workshops, ISACA brings a unique and valuable understanding of how to implement the Cybersecurity Framework. This understanding is presented through the guidance and templates provided in this document. For example, while the CSF provides references to important security controls, ISACA processes help to apply them through concepts such as the COBIT goals cascade. The goals cascade supports identification of stakeholder needs and enterprise goals, achieved by technical outcomes, which, in turn, support successful use of enabling processes and organizational structures. Through provision of practical processes, the reader is, in this way, guided to attain CSF outcomes in a more measurable way than without these underlying processes. This application will result in an organization that understands potential risk (and associated potential impacts) and is prepared to deal with unforeseen circumstances, helping to minimize losses and gain a business advantage.

Chapter 1. Introduction

Background

Threats to information security systems are not new; ISACA was incorporated nearly fifty years ago to address the need for a centralized source of information and guidance for securing computer systems. Today's cybersecurity attacks portend more threatening ones ahead, as evidenced by recent disruptive denial-of-service attacks against the US financial industry that hampered 15 of the largest US banks for hundreds of hours.[1] Attackers are organized and well-supported, leveraging sophisticated methods that dwarf the hacker assaults of the early 21st century. At the same time, society is highly dependent on technology, and connectivity and information sharing are increasingly vital. As mobile devices continue to proliferate, and as the Internet of Things continues to evolve, the need to protect against cybersecurity attacks is increasingly important.

To help address these needs, ISACA has developed a new security knowledge platform and cybersecurity professional program. The Cybersecurity Nexus (CSX), developed in collaboration with cybersecurity experts from leading companies around the world, supplies cutting-edge thought leadership, training and certification programs for professionals who are leading cybersecurity to the future. As part of the knowledge, tools and guidance provided by CSX, ISACA has developed this guide for implementing the NIST *Framework for Improving Critical Infrastructure Cybersecurity* (the Cybersecurity Framework, or CSF).

While the CSF was originally created in support of critical infrastructure providers, it is applicable to any organization that wishes to better manage and reduce cybersecurity risk. Nearly all organizations, in some way, support critical infrastructure. Each is connected to critical functions and services as a consumer, through the global economy, through telecommunication services and in many other ways. Improved risk management by each implementer will, ultimately, reduce global cybersecurity risk.

This implementation guide addresses business and technical requirements to apply the CSF, leveraging selected documents, principles and practices such as those developed by the IT Governance Institute[2] (ITGI). The anticipated audience ranges from board and executive management to technical operators and maintenance personnel. **Figure 1** identifies several of the key roles/functions and the benefit each receives from the CSF. While these key roles are applicable across all sectors and industry, specific tailoring may be required to align with specific organizational roles and functions.

---

[1] Recent attacks against US banking infrastructure are described, for example, at *www.nbcnews.com/video/nightly-news/51435096* and *www.aba.com/Advocacy/Testimonies/Documents/Johnson%20Senate%20Testimony.pdf*.
[2] ITGI was formed by ISACA in 1998 to advance international thinking on Governance of Enterprise IT. More information is available at *www.itgi.org*.

Figure 1—CSF Implementation—Target Audience and Benefits		
Framework Role	**Role/Function**	**Benefit of/Reason for Applying the Framework**
Executive	Board and Executive Management	• Understanding of their responsibilities and roles in cybersecurity within the organization • Better understanding of current cybersecurity posture • Better understanding of cybersecurity risk to the organization • Better understanding of cybersecurity target state • Understanding of actions required to close gaps between current cybersecurity posture and target state
Business/Process	IT Management	• Awareness of business impacts • Understanding relationship of business systems and their associated risk appetite
Business/Process	IT Process Management	• Understanding of business requirements and mission objectives and their priorities
Business/Process	Risk Management	• Enhanced view of the operational environment to discern the likelihood of a cybersecurity event
Business/Process	Legal Experts	• Understanding of cyberthreats to the business units and their mission objectives • Understanding of all compliance requirements for each business unit
Implementation/ Operator	Implementation Team	• Understanding of security controls and their importance in managing operational security risk • Detailed understanding of required actions to close gaps in cybersecurity requirements
Implementation/ Operator	Employees	• Understanding of cybersecurity requirements for their associated business systems

Governance and Management of Enterprise Information Technology

ISACA is dedicated to supporting the knowledge and skills to help practitioners determine and achieve strategic goals and realize business benefits through the effective and innovative use of technology. In the context of this document, we will use the following terms to describe the plans, processes and activities:

• **Enterprise**—A group of individuals working together for a common purpose, typically within the context of an organizational form such as a corporation, public agency, charity or trust
• **Organization**—The structure or arrangement of related or connected components of an enterprise defined by a particular scope

- **Governance**—Ensures that stakeholder needs, conditions and options are evaluated to determine balanced, agreed-on enterprise objectives to be achieved; setting direction through prioritization and decision making; and monitoring performance and compliance against agreed-on direction and objectives
- **Management**—Planning, building, operating and monitoring activities, in alignment with the direction set by the governance body, to achieve the enterprise objectives

The ISACA documents referenced in this guide regularly reference "information technology," or IT. In the context of this guide, IT refers to the technical processes and solutions (hardware and software) that enable the business functions to achieve the enterprise objectives. It is important to note that, in this context, technology includes operational technology (OT) (e.g., automated machinery control systems) and traditional information technology (IT) (e.g., payroll or email systems). Technical systems are converging, and the systems that enable enterprise value are becoming increasingly connected. The programmable logic controllers that support a manufacturing process, for example, use similar computing devices to those that support office printing needs, and both have a need for effective cybersecurity governance and management processes.

Planning and management processes described in this implementation guide may be helpful to organizations in evaluating and supporting convergence of OT and IT. Throughout each of the steps in this guide, the reader is encouraged to adopt a comprehensive view of technology. For example, determining critical organizational assets uses COBIT 5 practice APO07.02 *Identify key IT personnel*. This activity often includes consideration of an important database administrator or data center operator, but should also include consideration of those who maintain important industrial control system (ICS) components, digital locks and cameras, or facility operations (phone, HVAC [heating, ventilation and air conditioning], electrical). A broad view of enterprise technology will help support effective cybersecurity management in all planning, building, operating and monitoring activities.

Introduction to the *Framework for Improving Critical Infrastructure Cybersecurity*

Recognizing the need for broad safeguards to protect the United States from cybersecurity attacks that could disrupt power, water, communication and other critical systems, US President Obama issued Executive Order (EO) 13636.[3] The EO directs the executive branch of the US government to collaborate with industrial partners around the world to work on the following initiatives:[4]
- Develop a technology-neutral voluntary cybersecurity framework.
- Promote and incentivize the adoption of cybersecurity practices.

---

[3] Executive Order (EO) 13636 is available from the US Government Printing Office at *www.gpo.gov/fdsys/pkg/FR-2013-02-19/pdf/2013-03915.pdf*
[4] Some of the EO 13636 information listed is drawn from the Department of Homeland Security's fact sheet for EO 13636 and PPD-21, available at *www.dhs.gov/sites/default/files/publications/EO-PPD%20Fact%20Sheet%2012March13.pdf.*

• Increase the volume, timeliness and quality of cyberthreat information sharing.
• Incorporate strong privacy and civil liberties protections into every initiative to secure our critical infrastructure.
• Explore the use of existing regulation to promote cybersecurity.

President Obama also created Presidential Policy Directive (PPD)-21: *Critical Infrastructure Security and Resilience* replacing Homeland Security Presidential Directive 7. It directs the executive branch of the US government to take the following actions for US critical infrastructure (listed in **figure 2**):
• Develop a situational awareness capability that addresses both physical and cyber aspects of how infrastructure is functioning in near-real time.
• Understand the cascading consequences of infrastructure failures.
• Evaluate and mature the public-private partnership.
• Update the National Infrastructure Protection Plan.
• Develop a comprehensive research and development plan.

Figure 2—Sector-specific Agencies as Described in PPD-21	
Sector	**Sector Specific Agency or Agencies**
Chemical	Department of Homeland Security
Commercial Facilities	Department of Homeland Security
Communications	Department of Homeland Security
Critical Manufacturing	Department of Homeland Security
Dams	Department of Homeland Security
Defense Industrial Base	Department of Defense
Emergency Services	Department of Homeland Security
Energy	Department of Energy
Financial Services	Department of the Treasury
Food and Agriculture	Departments of Agriculture and Health and Human Services
Government Facilities	Dept of Homeland Security and General Services Administration
Health Care and Public Health	Department of Health and Human Services
Information Technology	Department of Homeland Security
Nuclear Reactors, Materials and Waste	Department of Homeland Security
Transportation Systems	Departments of Homeland Security and Transportation
Water and Wastewater Systems	Environmental Protection Agency

Section 7 of EO 13636 directed the Secretary of Commerce to task NIST with leading development of a framework (the Cybersecurity Framework) to reduce cyberrisk to critical infrastructure. The CSF includes a set of standards, methodologies, procedures and processes that align policy, business and technological approaches to address cyberrisk. The EO directs NIST to incorporate voluntary consensus standards and industry best practices, and to be consistent with voluntary international standards when such international standards will advance the objectives of the EO.

The success criteria for the CSF were provided in section 7 of EO 13636. It requires that the CSF:
• Provide a prioritized, flexible, repeatable, performance-based and cost-effective approach, including information security measures and controls, to help owners and operators of critical infrastructure identify, assess and manage cyberrisk.
• Focus on identifying cross-sector security standards and guidelines applicable to critical infrastructure.
• Identify areas for improvement that should be addressed through future collaboration with particular sectors and standards-developing organizations.
• Provide guidance that is technology neutral and that enables critical infrastructure sectors to benefit from a competitive market for products and services that meet the standards, methodologies, procedures and processes developed to address cyberrisk.
• Include guidance for measuring the performance of an entity in implementing the Cybersecurity Framework.

In answer to this directive, NIST issued a request for information (RFI) in February 2013, asking a broad array of questions to gather relevant input from industry, academia and other stakeholders. NIST solicited information on how organizations assess risk; how cybersecurity factors into that risk assessment; the current usage of existing cybersecurity frameworks, standards and guidelines; and other management practices related to cybersecurity. In addition, NIST asked about legal/regulatory aspects of particular frameworks, standards, guidelines and/or best practices and the challenges organizations perceive in meeting such requirements.

NIST subsequently conducted five workshops throughout the United States to further refine industry feedback, including significant assistance from ISACA and its membership. Based on the responses to the RFI and results from the workshops, NIST provided a Cybersecurity Framework that identifies existing practices to inform an organization's risk management decisions related to the prevention and detection of, response to, and recovery from cybersecurity issues.

NIST released version 1.0 of the Cybersecurity Framework[5] on February 12, 2014. CSF 1.0 identifies three components: Framework Core, Framework Implementation Tiers and Framework Profiles. These three CSF elements are discussed in further detail in chapter 2.

---

[5] The NIST *Framework for Improving Critical Infrastructure Cybersecurity* may be downloaded at *www.nist.gov/cyberframework/upload/cybersecurity-framework-021214.pdf.*

Introduction to COBIT 5

COBIT 5 provides a comprehensive framework that assists enterprises in achieving their objectives for the governance and management of enterprise IT (GEIT). It may be implemented in a gradual approach, starting small and building on initial success, or managed in a holistic manner for the entire enterprise, taking in the full end-to-end business and IT functional areas of responsibility. In either approach, COBIT helps enterprises create optimal value from IT by maintaining a balance between realizing benefits and optimizing risk levels and resource use. COBIT 5 is generic and useful for enterprises of all sizes: commercial, not-for-profit or public sector. The COBIT 5 product family is shown in **figure 3**.

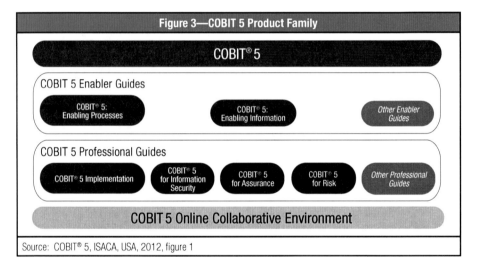

Source: COBIT® 5, ISACA, USA, 2012, figure 1

The COBIT 5 product family includes the following products:
• COBIT 5 (the framework)
• COBIT 5 enabler guides, in which governance and management enablers are discussed in detail. These include: *COBIT® 5: Enabling Processes; COBIT® 5: Enabling Information*; and other related enabling guides.
• COBIT 5 professional guides, which include:
  – *COBIT® 5 Implementation*
  – *COBIT® 5 for Information Security*
  – *COBIT® 5 for Assurance*
  – *COBIT® 5 for Risk*
  – Other professional guides

The COBIT 5 framework is based on five key principles for GEIT:
• Principle 1: Meeting Stakeholder Needs
• Principle 2: Covering the Enterprise End-to-end
• Principle 3: Applying a Single, Integrated Framework

• Principle 4: Enabling a Holistic Approach
• Principle 5: Separating Governance From Management

Together, these five principles enable the enterprise to build an effective governance and management framework that optimizes information and technology investment and use for the benefit of stakeholders.

Enterprises exist to create value for their stakeholders. Consequently, any enterprise will have value creation as a governance objective. Value creation means realizing benefits at an optimal resource cost while optimizing risk. Benefits can take many forms, e.g., financial for commercial enterprises or taxpayer benefits and improved public service for government entities.

COBIT 5 Governance and Management
The COBIT 5 framework makes a clear distinction between governance and management. These two disciplines encompass different types of activities, require different organizational structures and serve different purposes. The COBIT 5 view on this key distinction between governance and management is:
• **Governance**—Governance ensures that stakeholder needs, conditions and options are evaluated to determine balanced, agreed-on enterprise objectives to be achieved; setting direction through prioritization and decision making; and monitoring performance and compliance against agreed-on direction and objectives.
• **Management**—Management plans, builds, runs and monitors activities in alignment with the direction set by the governance body to achieve the enterprise objectives.

COBIT 5 Goals Cascade
Stakeholder needs have to be transformed into an enterprise's actionable strategy. The COBIT 5 goals cascade is the mechanism to translate stakeholder needs into specific, actionable and customized enterprise goals, IT-related goals and enabler goals. This translation allows setting specific goals at every level and in every area of the enterprise in support of the overall goals and stakeholder requirements, and thus effectively supports alignment between enterprise needs and IT solutions and services.

COBIT 5 Enablers
COBIT 5 provides a holistic and systemic view on GEIT, based on a number of enablers. Enablers are factors that, individually and collectively, influence whether something will work—in this case, governance and management over enterprise IT. Enablers are driven by the goals cascade, i.e., higher-level IT-related goals define what the different enablers should achieve.
The COBIT 5 framework describes seven categories of enablers:
• Principles, policies and frameworks
• Processes

• Organizational structures
• Culture, ethics and behavior
• Information
• Services, infrastructure and applications
• People, skills and competencies

Any enterprise must always consider an interconnected set of enablers. Each enabler:
• Needs the input of other enablers to be fully effective, e.g., processes need information, organizational structures need skills and behavior
• Delivers output to the benefit of other enablers, e.g., processes deliver information, skills and behavior make processes efficient

COBIT 5 Process Reference Model

Processes are one of the seven enabler categories for GEIT. COBIT 5 includes a process reference model, defining and describing in detail a number of governance and management processes. It provides a process reference model that represents all of the processes that relate to IT activities normally found in an enterprise, offering a common reference model understandable to operational IT and business managers. The proposed process model is a complete, comprehensive model, but it is not the only possible process model. Each enterprise must define its own process set, taking into account the specific situation.

Incorporating an operational model and a common language for all parts of the enterprise involved in IT activities is one of the most important and critical steps toward good governance. It also provides a framework for measuring and monitoring IT performance, communicating with service providers, and integrating best management practices.

COBIT 5 advocates that the enterprise implement governance and management processes such that the key areas are covered, shown in **figure 4**.

Figure 5 shows the complete set of 37 governance and management processes within COBIT 5. The details of all processes are included in *COBIT 5: Enabling Processes.*

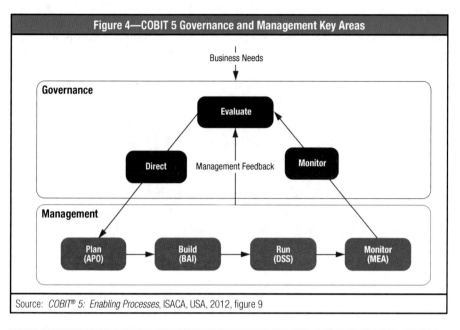

Figure 4—COBIT 5 Governance and Management Key Areas

Source: *COBIT® 5: Enabling Processes*, ISACA, USA, 2012, figure 9

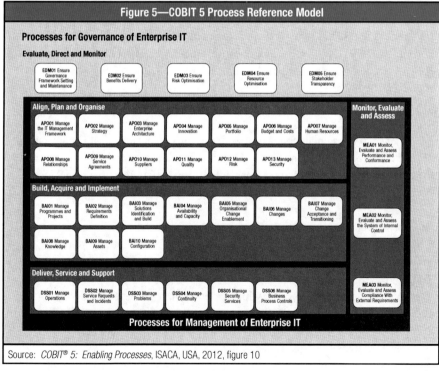

Figure 5—COBIT 5 Process Reference Model

Source: *COBIT® 5: Enabling Processes*, ISACA, USA, 2012, figure 10

COBIT 5 Implementation Guidance

Optimal value can be realized from leveraging COBIT only if it is effectively adopted and adapted to suit each enterprise's unique environment. Each implementation approach will also need to address specific challenges, including managing changes to culture and behavior.

ISACA provides practical and extensive implementation guidance in its publication *COBIT 5 Implementation*, which is based on a continual improvement life cycle. It is not intended to be a prescriptive approach nor a complete solution, but rather a guide to avoid commonly encountered pitfalls, leverage good practices and assist in the creation of successful outcomes. The guide is also supported by an implementation tool kit containing a variety of resources that will be continually enhanced. Its content includes:
• Self-assessment, measurement and diagnostic tools
• Presentations aimed at various audiences
• Related articles and further explanations

The following are important topics covered in *COBIT 5 Implementation*:
• Making a business case for the implementation and improvement of the governance and management of IT
• Recognizing typical pain points and trigger events
• Creating the appropriate environment for implementation
• Leveraging COBIT to identify gaps and guide the development of enablers such as policies, processes, principles, organizational structures, and roles and responsibilities.

Scope and Approach

The guidance in this publication is intended to assist organizations with understanding steps for CSF implementation using ISACA methods and approach. The guide provides processes, example templates and guidance for using CSF to identify and achieve enterprise and organizational objectives for the governance and management of IT.

The information is organized as follows:
• **Chapter 2**—Provides a detailed introduction into the NIST Cybersecurity Framework 1.0 and its three components: Framework Core, Implementation Tiers and Profiles
• **Chapter 3**—Describes approach, with supporting templates, for implementing the CSF to holistically improve GEIT
• **Chapter 4**—Illustrates the use of the CSF to communicate cybersecurity requirements among internal and external stakeholders
• **Appendix A:** Framework Core—Provides a copy of the Framework Core for quick reference

- **Appendix B:** Profile Template—Provides an overview of the profile template used to collect information regarding the current state and target state of the organizations cybersecurity program
- **Appendix C:** Framework Cover Letter—Provides a copy of the initial message released to senior executives to outline the goals and intent of the CSF
- **Appendix D:** Action Planning—Provides considerations for developing an action plan for tracking gap closing actions
- **Appendix E:** Considerations for Critical Infrastructure Sectors—Provides considerations and priorities for tailoring CSF implementation

Figure 6 provides an overview of this document and the location of information to answer common questions regarding the implementation of the CSF.

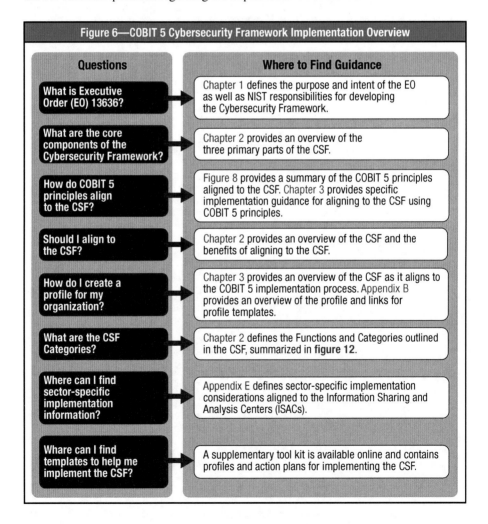

Figure 6—COBIT 5 Cybersecurity Framework Implementation Overview

Questions	Where to Find Guidance
What is Executive Order (EO) 13636?	Chapter 1 defines the purpose and intent of the EO as well as NIST responsibilities for developing the Cybersecurity Framework.
What are the core components of the Cybersecurity Framework?	Chapter 2 provides an overview of the three primary parts of the CSF.
How do COBIT 5 principles align to the CSF?	Figure 8 provides a summary of the COBIT 5 principles aligned to the CSF. Chapter 3 provides specific implementation guidance for aligning to the CSF using COBIT 5 principles.
Should I align to the CSF?	Chapter 2 provides an overview of the CSF and the benefits of aligning to the CSF.
How do I create a profile for my organization?	Chapter 3 provides an overview of the CSF as it aligns to the COBIT 5 implementation process. Appendix B provides an overview of the profile and links for profile templates.
What are the CSF Categories?	Chapter 2 defines the Functions and Categories outlined in the CSF, summarized in **figure 12**.
Where can I find sector-specific implementation information?	Appendix E defines sector-specific implementation considerations aligned to the Information Sharing and Analysis Centers (ISACs).
Whare can I find templates to help me implement the CSF?	A supplementary tool kit is available online and contains profiles and action plans for implementing the CSF.

Page intentionally left blank

Chapter 2. Introduction to NIST Cybersecurity Framework 1.0

Framework Background

The CSF was developed in response to US Presidential Executive Order 13636, which states,

> *"Repeated cyber intrusions into critical infrastructure demonstrate the need for improved cybersecurity. The cyber threat to critical infrastructure continues to grow and represents one of the most serious national security challenges we must confront."*

The goals of the EO align well with the COBIT 5 framework, which recognizes that "information is a key resource for all enterprises," and "information technology is increasingly advanced and has become pervasive in enterprises and in social, public and business environments." The ISACA publication points out that

> *"COBIT 5 helps enterprises to create optimal value from IT by maintaining a balance between realizing benefits and optimizing risk levels and resource use. COBIT 5 enables IT to be governed and managed in a holistic manner for the entire enterprise, taking into account the full end-to-end business and IT functional areas of responsibility and considering the IT-related interests of internal and external stakeholders."*

Over a one-year process, staff from NIST met with industry partners to consider responses to the February 2013 RFI, and further refined guidance to create a risk-based framework for reducing risk.

Workshop participation and comment submissions included significant contribution from small- and medium-sized businesses (SMBs), and from the international business community. This diversity of input greatly improved the understanding of the challenges and root causes underlying modern cybersecurity risk. The diverse support from SMBs contributed to a broad and flexible framework. Each RFI response and each subsequent workshop comment was reviewed and analyzed by NIST. Through analysis of response coverage across critical infrastructure sectors and organization types and consideration of terms and phrases that identified key response points, NIST identified commonalities and recurring themes (described in **figure 7**). These themes were leveraged and incorporated through the CSF during its development.

Figure 7—NIST Initial Framework Considerations			
Categories	**Framework Principles**	**Common Points**	**Initial Gaps**
Themes	• Flexibility • Impact on global operations • Risk management approaches • Leverage existing approaches, standards and best practices	• Senior management engagement • Understanding threat environment • Business risk/risk assessment • Separation of business and operational systems • Models/levels of maturity • Incident response • Cybersecurity workforce	• Metrics • Privacy/civil liberties • Tools • Dependencies • Industry best practices • Resiliency • Critical infrastructure cybersecurity nomenclature
Source: NIST, *2013 Initial Analysis of Cybersecurity Framework RFI Responses*, USA, figure 1, http://csrc.nist.gov/cyberframework/nist-initial-analysis-of-rfi-responses.pdf			

The CSF is a risk-based approach to managing cybersecurity risk and is comprised of three parts: the Framework Core, the Framework Implementation Tiers and the Framework Profiles. Each CSF component reinforces the connection between business drivers and cybersecurity activities.[6]

The Framework Core (detailed later in this document) is a set of cybersecurity activities, desired outcomes and applicable references that are common across critical infrastructure sectors. The Framework Implementation Tiers provide context on how an organization views cybersecurity risk and the processes in place to manage that risk. Tiers describe the degree to which an organization's cybersecurity risk management practices exhibit the characteristics defined in the Framework (e.g., risk- and threat-aware, repeatable, and adaptive). The Tiers characterize an organization's practices over a range, from Partial (Tier 1) to Adaptive (Tier 4). A Framework Profile represents the outcomes based on business needs that an organization has selected from the Framework Categories and Subcategories. The Profile can be characterized as the alignment of standards, guidelines and practices to the Framework Core in a particular implementation scenario. Profiles can be used to identify opportunities for improving cybersecurity posture by comparing a Current Profile (the "as is" state) with a Target Profile (the "to be" state).

In addition to providing a Cybersecurity Framework, the *Framework for Improving Critical Infrastructure Cybersecurity* also provides basic implementation guidance through a seven-step process.

---

[6] NIST, *Framework for Improving Critical Infrastructure Cybersecurity*, www.nist.gov/cyberframework/upload/cybersecurity-framework-021214.pdf

- **Step 1: Prioritize and Scope**—Requests that organizations scope and prioritize business/mission objectives and high-level organizational priorities. This information allows organizations to make strategic decisions regarding the scope of systems and assets that support the selected business lines or processes within the organization.
- **Step 2: Orient**—Provides organizations an opportunity to identify threats to, and vulnerabilities of, systems identified in the Prioritize and Scope step.
- **Step 3: Create a Current Profile**—Identifies the requirement to define the current state of the organization's cybersecurity program by establishing a current state profile.
- **Step 4: Conduct a Risk Assessment**—Allows organizations to conduct a risk assessment using their currently accepted methodology. The information used from this step in the process is used in Step 5.
- **Step 5: Create a Target Profile**—Allows organizations to develop a risk-informed target state profile. The target state profile focuses on the assessment of the Framework Categories and Subcategories describing the organization's desired cybersecurity outcomes.
- **Step 6: Determine, Analyze, and Prioritize Gaps**—Organizations conduct a gap analysis to determine opportunities for improving the current state. The gaps are identified by overlaying the current state profile with the target state profile.
- **Step 7: Implement Action Plan**—After the gaps are identified and prioritized, the required actions are taken to close the gaps and work toward obtaining the target state.

While hundreds of organizations provided input into the design of the Cybersecurity Framework, ISACA was deeply engaged in the CSF development at each stage. Many ISACA principles are visible in the CSF implementation steps. **Figure 8** illustrates some parallels between CSF implementation steps and COBIT 5 framework principles.

Figure 8—Comparison of CSF Implementation Steps With COBIT 5 Principles	
CSF Implementation Steps	**COBIT 5 Principles**
Step 1: Prioritize and Scope—Directs implementers to identify business/mission objectives and high-level organizational priorities. This mission understanding is critical to ensure that resulting risk decisions are prioritized and aligned with stakeholder goals, ensuring effective risk management and optimizing investment.	**Principle 1: Meeting Stakeholder Needs**—Enterprises exist to create value for their stakeholders by maintaining a balance between the realization of benefits and the optimization of risk and use of resources. An enterprise can customize COBIT 5 to suit its own context through the goals cascade, translating high-level enterprise goals into manageable, specific goals and map these to specific processes and practices.

Figure 8—Comparison of CSF Implementation Steps With COBIT 5 Principles *(cont.)*	
CSF Implementation Steps	**COBIT 5 Principles**
Step 2: Orient—The organization identifies an overall risk approach, considering enterprise people, processes and technology along with external drivers such as regulatory requirements. It identifies threats to, and vulnerabilities of, those assets. **Step 3: Create a Current Profile**—Through use of a Profile template (example provided later in this publication) the organization determines the current state of Category and Subcategory outcomes from the Framework Core (analogous to COBIT 5 governance and management enablers) and how each is currently being achieved. **Step 4: Conduct a Risk Assessment**—The organization, guided by its risk management process, analyzes the operational environment to discern the likelihood of a cybersecurity event and the impact that the event could have. Incorporate emerging risk, threat, and vulnerability data to facilitate a robust understanding of the likelihood and impact of cybersecurity events. **Step 5: Create a Target Profile**—The organization creates a Target Profile that focuses on the assessment of the Framework Categories and Subcategories describing the organization's desired cybersecurity outcomes. The organizations may develop additional Categories and Subcategories to account for unique organizational risk. It may also consider influences and requirements of external stakeholders such as sector entities, customers and business partners when creating a Target Profile. **Step 6: Determine, Analyze, and Prioritize Gaps**—The organization compares Current and Target Profiles to determine gaps. It creates a prioritized action plan to address those gaps, drawing on mission drivers, cost/benefit analysis, and risk understanding to achieve the target outcomes. The organization determines the resources necessary to address the gaps.	**Principle 2: Covering the Enterprise End-to-end**—COBIT 5 integrates governance of enterprise IT into enterprise governance: • It covers all functions and processes within the enterprise; COBIT 5 does not focus only on the "IT function," but treats information and related technologies as assets that need to be dealt with just like any other asset by everyone in the enterprise. • It considers all IT-related governance and management enablers to be enterprisewide and end-to-end, i.e., inclusive of everything and everyone—internal and external—that is relevant to governance and management of enterprise information and related IT. **Principle 3: Applying a Single, Integrated Framework**—There are many IT-related standards and good practices, each providing guidance on a subset of IT activities. COBIT 5 aligns with other relevant standards and frameworks at a high level, and thus can serve as the overarching framework for governance and management of enterprise IT.

Figure 8—Comparison of CSF Implementation Steps With COBIT 5 Principles *(cont.)*	
CSF Implementation Steps	**COBIT 5 Principles**
Step 7: Implement Action Plan—The organization determines which actions to take in regard to the gaps, if any, identified in the previous step. It then monitors its current cybersecurity practices against the Target Profile. For further guidance, the CSF identifies example Informative References regarding the Categories and Subcategories, but organizations should determine which standards, guidelines and practices, including those that are sector-specific, work best for their needs. An organization may repeat the steps as needed to continuously assess and improve its cybersecurity. For instance, organizations may find that more frequent repetition of the Orient step improves the quality of risk assessments. Furthermore, organizations may monitor progress through iterative updates to the current profile, subsequently comparing the Current Profile to the Target Profile. Organizations may utilize this process to align their cybersecurity program with their desired Implementation Tier.	**Principle 4: Enabling a Holistic Approach**—Efficient and effective governance and management of enterprise IT require a holistic approach, taking into account several interacting components. COBIT 5 defines a set of enablers to support the implementation of a comprehensive governance and management system for enterprise IT. Enablers are broadly defined as anything that can help to achieve the objectives of the enterprise. The COBIT 5 framework defines seven categories of enablers: 1. Principles, Policies and Frameworks 2. Processes 3. Organizational Structures 4. Culture, Ethics and Behavior 5. Information 6. Services, Infrastructure and Applications 7. People, Skills and Competencies
COBIT 5 Principle 5 is not directly embedded and may represent an opportunity for improvement for the CSF.	**Principle 5: Separating Governance From Management**—The COBIT 5 framework makes a clear distinction between governance and management. These two disciplines encompass different types of activities, require different organizational structures and serve different purposes.

Coordination of Framework Implementation

Another important aspect of the CSF is its guidance regarding stakeholder communications. NIST's analysis of industry feedback during the development period indicated that risk decisions, in many organizations, were not well aligned with enterprise drivers and goals. As *COBIT 5 for Risk* points out, when risk capacity and risk appetite are defined by board and executive management at the enterprise level (see COBIT 5 process EDM03 *Ensure risk optimization*), the prioritization and approval process of risk response actions are improved.

The CSF common flow of information and decisions at the following levels within an organization are similar to those described in COBIT 5's stakeholder roles, shown in **figure 9**.

Figure 9—Comparison of CSF and COBIT Roles	
CSF Role	**COBIT 5 Role**
Executive Level	Board of directors and executive management
Business/Process	Business management and business process owners
Implementation/Operations	IT management and IT process owners (e.g., head of operations, chief architect, IT security manager, business continuity management specialist) and other implementation team members

The executive level communicates information about enterprise goals and mission priorities, using language, approaches and communications that are meaningful to executive management. This activity is comparable to the COBIT implementation phase "Phase 1—What Are the Drivers?" Dialogue with business management and business process owners includes definition of appropriate risk tolerances and available resources. The business/process level, in turn, uses the information as inputs into the risk management process, and then collaborates with the IT management and IT process owners to communicate business needs.

These two levels of management determine the current cybersecurity state using a Framework Profile template (described later in this document.) The Current Profile and Target Profile provide considerations comparable to COBIT's next two implementation phases, "Phase 2—Where Are We Now?" and "Phase 3—Where Do We Want To Be?" Through comparison of the target with the current state, the implementation team is able to recommend specific and prioritized actions to achieve stakeholder goals, aligned with the phase 1 business drivers, resource requirements and organizational risk appetite. This action plan, comparable to COBIT implementation phases 4 and 5, "Phase 4—What Needs To Be Done?" and "Phase 5—"How Do We Get There?", provides a cost-effective, agile governance of enterprise IT approach that is scalable to any size organization.

As **figure 10** illustrates, the information flow is cyclical, with ongoing monitoring as a critical step. The COBIT implementation phases "Phase 6—Did We Get There?" and "Phase 7—How Do We Keep the Momentum Going?" provide important considerations to ensure ongoing, cost-effective governance and management. For example, as technical changes occur (e.g., changes to physical, process and technical assets; updated threats; discovered or remediated vulnerabilities), the implementation/operations level communicates the Profile implementation progress to the business/process level.

The business/process level uses this information to perform an impact assessment in consideration of the business drivers. Business/process level management reports the outcomes of that impact assessment to the executive level, using language and methods appropriate for the board of directors/executive management communications, to inform the organization's overall risk management process.

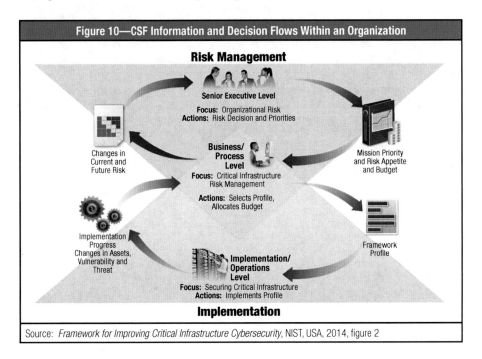

Figure 10—CSF Information and Decision Flows Within an Organization

Source: *Framework for Improving Critical Infrastructure Cybersecurity*, NIST, USA, 2014, figure 2

Framework Core

The Framework Core is a set of cybersecurity activities, desired outcomes and applicable references that are common across critical infrastructure sectors. The Core presents industry standards, guidelines and practices in a manner that allows for communication of cybersecurity activities and outcomes across the organization from the executive level to the implementation/operations level. The Framework Core consists of five concurrent and continuous Functions—Identify, Protect, Detect, Respond, Recover. When considered together, these Functions provide a high-level, strategic view of the life cycle of an organization's management of cybersecurity risk. The Framework Core then identifies underlying key Categories and Subcategories for each Function, and matches them with example Informative References such as existing standards, guidelines and practices for each Subcategory, as depicted in **figure 11**.

The outcomes in the Core help the reader to answer the following questions:

- What people, processes and technologies are essential to provide the right services to the right stakeholders?
- What do we need to do to protect those assets from the risk discovered in the Identify function?
- What detection capability can we implement to recognize potential or realized risk to organizational assets from identified risk?
- What response and recovery activities are appropriate and necessary to continue operations (albeit diminished) or restore services described above?

Figure 11—Components of the Framework Core

Functions	Categories	Subcategories	Informative References
IDENTIFY			
PROTECT			
DETECT			
RESPOND			
RECOVER			

Source: *Framework for Improving Critical Infrastructure Cybersecurity*, NIST, USA, 2014, figure 1

CSF describes the five Core functions as follows:

- **Identify**—Develop the organizational understanding to manage cybersecurity risk to systems, assets, data and capabilities.

The activities in the Identify Function are foundational for effective use of the Framework. Understanding the business context, the resources that support critical functions and the related cybersecurity risk enables an organization to focus and prioritize its efforts, consistent with its risk management strategy and business needs. Examples of outcome Categories within this Function include: Asset Management; Business Environment; Governance; Risk Assessment; and Risk Management Strategy.

- **Protect**—Develop and implement the appropriate safeguards to ensure delivery of critical infrastructure services.

  The Protect Function supports the ability to limit or contain the impact of a potential cybersecurity event. Examples of outcome Categories within this Function include: Access Control; Awareness and Training; Data Security; Information Protection Processes and Procedures; Maintenance; and Protective Technology.
- **Detect**—Develop and implement the appropriate activities to identify the occurrence of a cybersecurity event.

  The Detect Function enables timely discovery of cybersecurity events. Examples of outcome Categories within this Function include: Anomalies and Events; Security Continuous Monitoring; and Detection Processes.
- **Respond**—Develop and implement the appropriate activities to take action regarding a detected cybersecurity event.

  The Respond Function supports the ability to contain the impact of a potential cybersecurity event. Examples of outcome Categories within this Function include: Response Planning; Communications; Analysis; Mitigation; and Improvements.
- **Recover**—Develop and implement the appropriate activities to maintain plans for resilience and to restore any capabilities or services that were impaired due to a cybersecurity event.

  The Recover Function supports timely recovery to normal operations to reduce the impact from a cybersecurity event. Examples of outcome Categories within this Function include: Recovery Planning; Improvements; and Communications.

Each Function is comprised of one or more Categories, process-specific outcomes that support cybersecurity management. These Categories, in turn, are comprised of numerous specific Subcategories that provide process assessment to determine current state and target goals. **Figure 12** provides an overview of the Framework Categories.

While many organizations maintain internal processes and procedures to achieve the outcomes instantiated by the Framework Core, others requested specific guidance as to how to gain that achievement. As illustrative examples of practices which some organizations use to achieve the outcomes, NIST provided informative references to cross-sector, internationally recognized guidance (including COBIT 5) that assist in accomplishing each Subcategory.

Function Unique Identifier	Function	Category Unique Identifier	Category
ID	Identify	AM	Asset Management
		BE	Business Environment
		GV	Governance
		RA	Risk Assessment
		RM	Risk Management
PR	Protect	AC	Access Control
		AT	Awareness and Training
		DS	Data Security
		IP	Information Protection Processes and Information
		PT	Protective Technology
DE	Detect	AE	Anomalies and Events
		CM	Security Continuous Monitoring
		DP	Detection Processes
RS	Respond	CO	Communications
		AN	Analysis
		MI	Mitigation
		IM	Improvements
RC	Recover	RP	Recovery Planning
		IM	Improvements
		CO	Communications

Figure 12—Framework Core Identifiers and Categories

Source: *Framework for Improving Critical Infrastructure Cybersecurity*, NIST, USA, 2014, Table 1

Framework Implementation Tiers

The CSF includes several levels of Implementation Tiers that assist in conducting assessment and planning of cybersecurity activities. The Tiers describe attributes to consider when creating a Target Profile or completing a Current Profile. The Tiers are described in detail in **figure 13**. While not considered a maturity model, the Tier characteristics describe a progression from *ad hoc* to adaptive in three categories:

- **Risk Management Process**—Considers the level to which the organizational cybersecurity risk management practices are formalized and institutionalized. The attributes consider the extent to which prioritization of cybersecurity activities are informed by organizational risk objectives, the threat environment and stakeholder requirements.
- **Integrated Risk Management Program**—Reviews the cybersecurity risk awareness at the organizational level. Levels increase as risk-informed, management-approved processes and procedures are defined and implemented and as they are adapted based on information sharing and lessons learned from previous activities.

• **External Participation**—Considers the level to which the organization actively shares information with external partners to improve security before a security event occurs and informs those partners about indicators, observations or events

Figure 13—Framework Implementation Tiers			
Tier	Risk Management Process	Integrated Risk Management Program	External Participation
Tier 1: Partial	Organizational cybersecurity risk management practices are not formalized, and risk is managed in an *ad hoc* and sometimes reactive manner. Prioritization of cybersecurity activities may not be directly informed by organizational risk objectives, the threat environment or business/mission requirements.	There is limited awareness of cybersecurity risk at the organizational level and an organizationwide approach to managing cybersecurity risk has not been established. The organization implements cybersecurity risk management on an irregular, case-by-case basis due to varied experience or information gained from outside sources. The organization may not have processes that enable cybersecurity information to be shared within the organization.	An organization may not have the processes in place to participate in coordination or collaboration with other entities.
Tier 2: Risk Informed	Risk management practices are approved by management but may not be established as organizationwide policy. Prioritization of cybersecurity activities is directly informed by organizational risk objectives, the threat environment or business/ mission requirements.	There is an awareness of cybersecurity risk at the organizational level but an organizationwide approach to managing cybersecurity risk has not been established. Risk-informed, management-approved processes and procedures are defined and implemented, and staff has adequate resources to perform their cybersecurity duties. Cybersecurity information is shared within the organization on an informal basis.	The organization knows its role in the larger ecosystem, but has not formalized its capabilities to interact and share information externally.

	Figure 13—Framework Implementation Tiers (cont.)		
Tier	**Risk Management Process**	**Integrated Risk Management Program**	**External Participation**
Tier 3: Repeatable	The organization's risk management practices are formally approved and expressed as policy. Organizational cybersecurity practices are regularly updated based on the application of risk management processes to changes in business/mission requirements and a changing threat and technology landscape.	There is an organizationwide approach to manage cybersecurity risk. Risk-informed policies, processes and procedures are defined, implemented as intended and reviewed. Consistent methods are in place to respond effectively to changes in risk. Personnel possess the knowledge and skills to perform their appointed roles and responsibilities.	The organization understands its dependencies and partners and receives information from these partners that enables collaboration and risk-based management decisions within the organization in response to events.
Tier 4: Adaptive	The organization adapts its cybersecurity practices based on lessons learned and predictive indicators derived from previous and current cybersecurity activities. Through a process of continuous improvement incorporating advanced cybersecurity technologies and practices, the organization actively adapts to a changing cybersecurity landscape and responds to evolving and sophisticated threats in a timely manner.	There is an organizationwide approach to managing cybersecurity risk that uses risk-informed policies, processes and procedures to address potential cybersecurity events. Cybersecurity risk management is part of the organizational culture and evolves from an awareness of previous activities, information shared by other sources and continuous awareness of activities on their systems and networks.	The organization manages risk and actively shares information with partners to ensure that accurate, current information is being distributed and consumed to improve cybersecurity before a cybersecurity event occurs.

It is noteworthy that the CSF provides neither descriptive guidance regarding how to measure these attributes, nor a quantitative method to determine the applicable Tier. NIST received numerous comments during the development process, many supporting a maturity model similar to that used in Electricity Subsector Cybersecurity Capability Maturity Model (ES-C2M2). Strict criteria are difficult, however, across a broad array of users, and NIST is not authoritative for deciding mandatory thresholds. For that reason, the Tiers are subjective, but help an organization consider current risk management practices, threat environment, legal and regulatory requirements, business/mission objectives, and organizational constraints. The lack of a concrete measurement standard in CSF version 1.0 is not intended to prevent such measurement; organizations (and organized groups, such as critical infrastructure sectors) may develop criteria to aid in comparison and communication of Tier selection.

The Framework Implementation Tiers are similar to COBIT's process capability levels (PCLs). While PCLs are assessed (in accordance with the COBIT Process Assessment Model [PAM] publication) at the individual process, the tiers apply to the organization itself, or a sub-component of the organization, depending on the scope of the implementation. Considerations of the PCLs may assist with determining the appropriate Framework tier.

Rating the outcomes described in **figure 13** will require professional judgment by the implementer. The reasons for selecting a tier, and for agreeing/disagreeing with an outcome statement in the Profiles, should be clearly documented so that advice can be given on areas in which the processes can be improved.

Specifically, the tiers compare in the following ways:
• **CSF Tier 1 (Partial)** is analogous to PCLs 0 (Incomplete) and 1 (Performed). At this level, the risk management and information sharing processes are either not implemented or are not yet formal enough to provide consistent organizational benefit.
• **CSF Tier 2 (Risk Informed)** is analogous to PCL 2 (Managed). The outcomes are now implemented in a managed fashion, informed by organizational risk processes and providing significant organizational awareness of cybersecurity risk management.
• **CSF Tier 3 (Repeatable)** is analogous to PCL 3 (Established). The managed process is now implemented using a defined method that is capable of achieving intended outcomes.
• **CSF Tier 4 (Adaptive)** is comparable to PCL 4 (Predictable) and PCL 5 (Optimizing). The outcomes are achieved proactively, learning from the experience of internal and external stakeholders, perhaps informed through external information sources. At PCL 5, the activities to accomplish given outcomes are continuously improved to meet relevant current and projected business goals in an optimal fashion.

The role of the Tiers in determining risk approach is closely related to COBIT's EDM03 *Ensure risk optimization*. As the organization adapts its cybersecurity practices based on lessons learned and predictive indicators, and as the organization builds an enterprise approach to risk management, the organization is better able to ensure identification and management of risk to the enterprise value. This in turn, enables the EDM03 goals of: ensuring that technology-related enterprise risk does not exceed risk appetite and risk tolerance, the impact of technology risk to enterprise value is identified and managed, and the potential for compliance failures is minimized.

Framework Profiles
A Framework Profile ("Profile") represents the outcomes based on business needs that an organization has selected from the Framework Categories and Subcategories. The Profile can be characterized as the alignment of standards, guidelines and practices to the Framework Core in a particular implementation scenario. Profiles can be used

to identify opportunities for improving cybersecurity posture by comparing a Current Profile (the "as is" state) with a Target Profile (the "to be" state). To develop a Profile, an organization can review each of the Core Categories and Subcategories and, based on business drivers and a risk assessment, determine which are most important; the organization adds Categories and Subcategories as needed to address its risk. The Current Profile can then be used to support prioritization and measurement of progress toward the Target Profile, factoring in business needs including cost-effectiveness and innovation. Profiles can be used to conduct self-assessments and to communicate within an organization or between organizations.

To assist organizations in adopting and implementing the Framework, CSF section 3.2 lays out a recommended seven-step implementation process. Each step is a precursor to the following step, although some organizations may conduct some steps in a different order. For example, an organization may adopt a Target Profile before performing a Current Profile, or might perform a risk assessment before developing a Current Profile. These steps, summarized and with detailed implementation recommendations described later in this guide, should be repeated as necessary to continuously improve an organization's cybersecurity.

Risk Considerations From COBIT and the CSF

Maintaining an understanding of enterprise security risk is a key component of the CSF. Step four of the CSF implementation process includes the requirement for performing a risk assessment. Risk assessments provide stakeholders and managers an opportunity to weigh security vulnerabilities, threats to the enterprise and technologies against operational requirements. Risk assessments assist in defining the subcategories required to adequately mitigate the risk to the organization and identify the rigor in which the mitigation should be applied. The rigor for implementing cybersecurity controls is attained through Implementation Tiers as described in CSF section 2.2.

The Institute of Risk Management (IRM) defines risk as "the combination of the probability of an event and its consequence. Consequences can range from positive to negative." The International Organization for Standardization defines risk in the internationally recognized ISO *Guide 73*, as the "effect of uncertainty on objectives," noting that an effect may be positive, negative or a deviation from the expected. In the context of applying the CSF, then, the primary consequence to be considered is the likelihood of achieving stakeholder goals. Similarly, *COBIT 5 for Risk* defines IT risk as business risk, specifically, the business risk associated with the use, ownership, operation, involvement, influence and adoption of IT within an enterprise. IT risk consists of IT-related events that could potentially impact the business. IT risk can occur with both uncertain frequency and impact, and creates challenges in meeting strategic goals and objectives. IT risk always exists, whether it is recognized by an enterprise.

As described in *COBIT 5 for Risk* and illustrated in **figure 14**, managed risk enables business drivers, enhances opportunities, and provides executives and managers with an understanding of the security strengths and weaknesses within the organization. When risk is poorly managed, business value is reduced, IT is misused, and executives and managers are unaware of potential security threats and vulnerabilities that could lead to lost revenue or reputation.

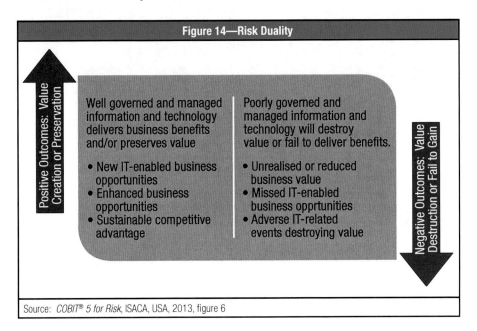

Figure 14—Risk Duality

Positive Outcomes: Value Creation or Preservation

Well governed and managed information and technology delivers business benefits and/or preserves value

- New IT-enabled business opportunities
- Enhanced business opportunities
- Sustainable competitive advantage

Poorly governed and managed information and technology will destroy value or fail to deliver benefits.

- Unrealised or reduced business value
- Missed IT-enabled business opprtunities
- Adverse IT-related events destroying value

Negative Outcomes: Value Destruction or Fail to Gain

Source: *COBIT® 5 for Risk*, ISACA, USA, 2013, figure 6

The Risk Function Perspective

COBIT 5 is an end-to-end framework that considers optimization of risk as a key value objective. COBIT 5 considers governance and management of risk as part of the overall GEIT. For each enabler, the risk function perspective describes how the enabler contributes to the overall risk governance and management function. For example, which:

- Processes are required to define and sustain the risk function, govern and manage risk—EDM01, APO01, etc.
- Information flows are required to govern and manage risk—risk universe, risk profile, etc.
- Organizational structures are required to govern and manage risk—ERM committee, risk function, etc.

Chapters 2 through 8 of *COBIT 5 for Risk* contain examples for each enabler. These examples are further elaborated in appendix B of *COBIT 5 for Risk*. The full scope of *COBIT 5 for Risk* is detailed in **figure 15**.

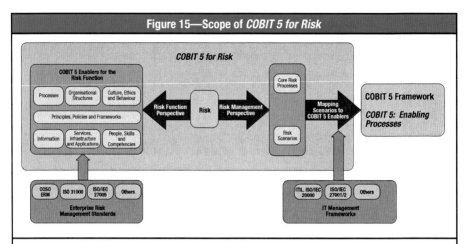

Figure 15—Scope of *COBIT 5 for Risk*

COBIT 5 for Risk provides specific guidance related to all enablers:
1. Risk **principles, policies and frameworks**
2. **Processes** including risk-function-specific details and activities
3. Risk-specific **organisational structures**
4. In terms of **culture, ethics and behaviour**, factors determining the success of risk governance
5. Risk-specific **information** types for enabling risk governance and management within the enterprise
6. With regard to **services, infrastructure and applications**, service capabilities required to provide risk and related functions to an enterprise.
7. For the **people, skills and competencies** enabler, skills and competencies specific for risk

Source: *COBIT® 5 for Risk,* ISACA, USA, 2013, figure 10

The Risk Management Perspective

The risk management perspective addresses governance and management, i.e., how to identify, analyze and respond to risk and how to use the COBIT 5 framework for that purpose. This perspective requires core risk processes (COBIT 5 processes EDM03 *Ensure risk optimization* and APO12 *Manage risk*) to be implemented.

The CSF leverages the risk assessment process to define how organizations will implement each Core Subcategory. Completing a risk assessment provides an understanding of the likelihood that a risk event will occur and what the resulting impact will be. For each potential event recorded above, determine the likelihood of that event occurring and the impact if it occurred. Organizations may choose to complete several risk assessments for each business area and aggregate the information to form enterprise risk assessments.

For some organizations, a separate risk assessment may be conducted for each business area (e.g. human resources, accounting, customer support) as defined by the Prioritize and Scope step. Separate risk assessments allow separate Target Profiles to ensure that the risk for the business area is addressed without overcompensating. The enterprise risk assessment provides a baseline to ensure that a minimum threshold is defined. This ensures that less sensitive business areas are not neglected and thus provide an avenue of attack for malicious users.

After the risk assessment is complete, organizations can determine the acceptable level of risk for IT assets and systems, expressed as their risk tolerance. The risk tolerance is used to define the controls required for each Subcategory and the rigor required for implementing the control by defining the target state profile.

Page intentionally left blank

Chapter 3. Framework Implementation

The following section describes the use of ISACA methodologies to accomplish the implementation guidance in the CSF "How To Use" chapter. CSF and COBIT each provide seven high-level steps, or phases. These generally align, although COBIT provides a postexecution assessment (Phase 6—Did We Get There?) and ongoing life cycle maintenance activities (Phase 7—How Do We Keep The Momentum Going?) that are implicit, but not fully described in the CSF. It is important to note that implementation is not an "all or nothing" endeavor. Those adopting the processes described may select whichever ones will assist in accomplishing enterprise goals. In this sense, the processes are available to select from, not a checklist to implement.

The following text describes the use of the CSF to accomplish the seven COBIT implementation phases, providing the following information about each phase:
• The purpose of the phase
• Key activities in the phase
• COBIT 5 practice(s) and process(es) that support(s) application of that phase (i.e., realization of the applicable CSF Core Category/Subcategory Outcome)

The activities and processes described are informative and may help the implementation team to determine what to do for each phase, but they are not prescriptive and they should be tailored to achieve individual organizational goals and approach.

Relationship of the COBIT 5 Goals Cascade to the CSF

The CSF recognizes that, because every organization faces unique challenges and opportunities, including having numerous internal and external stakeholders, each has unique requirements for governance and management activities. These stakeholders drive requirements for the enterprise, and thus the cybersecurity risk. As those requirements are set, the organization can use the COBIT 5 framework goals cascade to further refine those requirements.

The COBIT 5 framework describes the goals cascade as

> *"the mechanism to translate stakeholder needs into specific, actionable and customized enterprise goals, IT-related goals and enabler goals. This translation allows setting specific goals at every level and in every area of the enterprise in support of the overall goals and stakeholder requirements, and thus effectively supports alignment between enterprise needs and IT solutions and services."*

The COBIT 5 goals cascade is shown in **figure 16.**

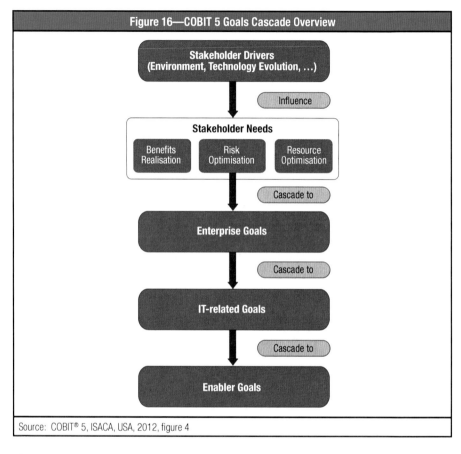

Figure 16—COBIT 5 Goals Cascade Overview

Source: COBIT® 5, ISACA, USA, 2012, figure 4

The goals cascade supports the identification of stakeholder needs and enterprise goals, which themselves contribute to understanding of the overall organizational drivers such as "compliance with external laws and regulations" or "business service continuity and availability." The achievement of enterprise goals is supported by technical outcomes, which, in turn, require successful application and use of a number of enablers. The enabler concept is detailed within the COBIT 5 framework. Enablers include processes, organizational structures and information, and for each enabler, a set of specific relevant goals defined in support of technical goals. In relation to the CSF, the enablers support activities to attain outcomes in the Core categories and subcategories.

An important note that was highlighted throughout CSF development workshops was that there may be layers of key stakeholders with varying enterprise goals. In the critical infrastructure community, for example, organizational goals may include drivers from national priorities, stakeholders from critical sector-specific agencies or officials from sector coordinating councils. These are not unlike existing enterprise goals, such as

"Compliance with external laws and regulations." Examining the organizational goals in this step should include understanding balanced priorities among what is best for the enterprise and any external commitments, such as provisioning of critical services.

CSF Step 1: Prioritize and Scope.
COBIT Phase 1—What Are the Drivers?

ITGI's governance guidance[7] for boards of directors and executive management points out that information security governance is the responsibility of the board of directors and senior executives. It must be an integral and transparent part of enterprise governance and be aligned with the IT governance framework. To exercise effective enterprise and information security governance, boards and senior executives must have a clear understanding of what to expect from their enterprise's information security program. This guidance was confirmed during the workshops leading to the development of the CSF. Reviewers pointed out that effective alignment of business drivers with GEIT resulted in improved security and better understanding of enterprise security requirements. GEIT's basis in mission supports the use of language and terminology that are familiar to the executive level, rather than the use of technical jargon and buzzwords that are misaligned with common business terms. Understanding of the governance issues and benefits, in business terms, supports buy-in and commitment from senior management.

Through these methods, accomplishment of the Core outcomes through selected organizational goals and processes directly support stakeholder goals and drivers, moving GEIT from merely a compliance exercise to a method to provide value to the organization.

Implementation Considerations
Purpose
To obtain an understanding of the organizational governance approach (including risk architecture, business drivers and compliance requirements) to inform risk assessment activities and to prioritize security activity
Inputs
• Enterprise policies, strategies, governance and business plans • Risk architecture strategy • Current enterprise environment and business processes • Enterprise vision and mission statements

---

[7] ITGI, *Information Security Governance: Guidance for Boards of Directors and Executive Management, 2nd Edition,* USA, 2006

Implementation Considerations *(cont.)*

High-level Activities

- Identify the key executive board-level stakeholders that authoritatively speak to mission drivers and risk appetite.
- Determine the scope to be addressed through application of the CSF. This level could be enterprisewide or any subsection of the organization.
- Identify organizational mission and/or services to be addressed through use of the CSF.
- Identify the applicable risk architecture for the organization and available methods for risk identification, measurement, assessment, reporting and monitoring.
- Define roles and responsibilities for conveying prioritization and resource availability, and for implementing actions to achieve IT value.
- Determine the systems (people, processes and technology) required to attain mission goals.
- Use the COBIT 5 goals cascade to translate stakeholder needs into specific, actionable and customized enterprise goals. This effectively supports alignment among enterprise needs and the CSF outcomes from subsequent phases, and aids in reporting progress toward goals.
- Document the prioritization decisions and resources available for managing risk to the appropriate level. Documentation should include accountability, deadlines and reporting method.

Outputs

- Enterprise architecture vision
- Organizational mission and drivers
- Organizational direction regarding funding and other resources
- Quality management system (QMS)
- Understanding of the enterprise's present and future attitude toward risk and IT risk position

Relevant COBIT 5 Practices	
COBIT 5 Practice	**Description**
EDM01.01	Evaluate the governance system. Continually identify and engage with the enterprise's stakeholders, document an understanding of the requirements, and make a judgment on the current and future design of governance of enterprise IT.
APO01 (all)	Provide a consistent management approach to enable the enterprise governance requirements to be met, covering management processes, organizational structures, roles and responsibilities, reliable and repeatable activities, and skills and competencies.
APO02.01	Understand enterprise direction. Consider the current enterprise environment and business processes, as well as the enterprise strategy and future objectives. Consider also the external environment of the enterprise (industry drivers, relevant regulations, basis for competition).
APO03.01	Develop the enterprise architecture vision. The architecture vision provides a first-cut, high-level description of the baseline and target architectures, covering the business, information, data, application and technology domains. The architecture vision provides the sponsor with a key tool to sell the benefits of the proposed capability to stakeholders within the enterprise. The architecture vision describes how the new capability will meet enterprise goals and strategic objectives and address stakeholder concerns when implemented.

Relevant COBIT 5 Practices *(cont.)*	
COBIT 5 Practice	**Description**
APO04.02	Maintain an understanding of the enterprise environment. Work with relevant stakeholders to understand their challenges. Maintain an adequate understanding of enterprise strategy and the competitive environment or other constraints so that opportunities enabled by new technologies can be identified.
APO05.01	Establish the target investment mix. Review and ensure clarity of the enterprise and IT strategies and current services. Define an appropriate investment mix based on cost; alignment with strategy; and financial measures such as cost and expected return on investment (ROI) over the full economic life cycle, degree of risk and type of benefit for the programs in the portfolio. Adjust the enterprise and IT strategies where necessary.
APO05.02	Determine the availability and sources of funds. Determine potential sources of funds, different funding options and the implications of the funding source on the investment return expectations.
APO05.03	Evaluate and select programs to fund. Based on the overall investment portfolio mix requirements, evaluate and prioritize program business cases, and decide on investment proposals. Allocate funds and initiate programs.
APO06.01	Manage finance and accounting. Establish and maintain a method to account for all IT-related costs, investments and depreciation as an integral part of the enterprise financial systems and chart of accounts to manage the investments and costs of IT. Capture and allocate actual costs, analyze variances between forecasts and actual costs, and report using the enterprise's financial measurement systems.
APO06.02	Prioritize resource allocation. Implement a decision-making process to prioritize the allocation of resources and rules for discretionary investments by individual business units. Include the potential use of external service providers and consider the buy, develop and rent options.
APO06.03	Create and maintain budgets. Prepare a budget reflecting the investment priorities supporting strategic objectives based on the portfolio of IT-enabled programs and IT services.
APO06.04	Model and allocate costs. Establish and use an IT costing model based on the service definition, ensuring that allocation of costs for services is identifiable, measurable and predictable, to encourage the responsible use of resources including those provided by service providers. Regularly review and benchmark the appropriateness of the cost/chargeback model to maintain its relevance and appropriateness to the evolving business and IT activities.
APO06.05	Manage costs. Implement a cost management process comparing actual costs to budgets. Costs should be monitored and reported and, in the case of deviations, identified in a timely manner and their impact on enterprise processes and services assessed.
APO07.01	Maintain adequate and appropriate staffing. Evaluate staffing requirements on a regular basis or on major changes to the enterprise or operational or IT environments to ensure that the enterprise has sufficient human resources to support enterprise goals and objectives. Staffing includes both internal and external resources.
APO08.01	Understand business expectations. Understand current business issues and objectives and business expectations for IT. Ensure that requirements are understood, managed and communicated, and their status agreed on and approved.

Relevant COBIT 5 Practices *(cont.)*	
COBIT 5 Practice	**Description**
APO08.03	Manage the business relationship. Manage the relationship with customers (business representatives). Ensure that relationship roles and responsibilities are defined and assigned, and communication is facilitated.
APO10.01	Identify and evaluate supplier relationships and contracts. Identify suppliers and associated contracts, then categorize them into type, significance and criticality. Establish supplier and contract evaluation criteria and evaluate the overall portfolio of existing and alternative suppliers and contracts.
APO10.02	Select suppliers. Select suppliers according to a fair and formal practice to ensure a viable best fit based on specified requirements. Requirements should be optimized with input from potential suppliers.
APO11.01	Establish a quality management system (QMS). Establish and maintain a QMS that provides a standard, formal and continuous approach to quality management for information, enabling technology and business processes that are aligned with business requirements and enterprise quality management.
APO11.03	Focus quality management on customers. Focus quality management on customers by determining their requirements and ensuring alignment with the quality management practices.
BAI01.01	Maintain a standard approach for program and project management. Maintain a standard approach for program and project management that enables governance and management review and decision-making and delivery management activities focused on achieving value and goals (requirements, risk, costs, schedule, quality) for the business in a consistent manner.
BAI01.02	Initiate a program. Initiate a program to confirm the expected benefits and obtain authorization to proceed. This includes agreeing on program sponsorship, confirming the program mandate through approval of the conceptual business case, appointing program board or committee members, producing the program brief, reviewing and updating the business case, developing a benefits realization plan, and obtaining approval from sponsors to proceed.
BAI01.03	Manage stakeholder engagement. Manage stakeholder engagement to ensure an active exchange of accurate, consistent and timely information that reaches all relevant stakeholders. This includes planning, identifying and engaging stakeholders and managing their expectations.
BAI01.04	Develop and maintain the program plan. Formulate a program to lay the initial groundwork and to position it for successful execution by formalizing the scope of the work to be accomplished and identifying the deliverables that will satisfy its goals and deliver value. Maintain and update the program plan and business case throughout the full economic life cycle of the program, ensuring alignment with strategic objectives and reflecting the current status and updated insights gained to date.

Relevant COBIT 5 Practices *(cont.)*	
COBIT 5 Practice	**Description**
BAI01.07	Start up and initiate projects within a program. Define and document the nature and scope of the project to confirm and develop among stakeholders a common understanding of project scope and how it relates to other projects within the overall IT-enabled investment program. The definition should be formally approved by the program and project sponsors.
BAI01.08	Plan projects. Establish and maintain a formal, approved integrated project plan (covering business and IT resources) to guide project execution and control throughout the life of the project. The scope of projects should be clearly defined and tied to building or enhancing business capability.
BAI01.09	Manage program and project quality. Prepare and execute a quality management plan, processes and practices, aligned with the QMS that describes the program and project quality approach and how it will be implemented. The plan should be formally reviewed and agreed on by all parties concerned and then incorporated into the integrated program and project plans.

CSF Step 2: Orient, and Step 3: Create a Current Profile
COBIT Phase 2—Where Are We Now?

Having identified the organizational mission and drivers that support stakeholder objectives, the organization identifies related systems and assets that enable achieving those stakeholder needs. It is important to note that the CSF does not limit these systems and assets to purely IT or OT, which are subsets of the overall list of assets to be considered. Examples of assets to consider in the Orient step include: facilities in which technology resides, operators that ensure equipment functions safely and infrastructure that delivers products to customers. Having gained an understanding of the cascading goals, and how the business and IT function need to deliver value from IT in support of the enterprise goals, the organization then identifies threats to, and vulnerabilities of, those systems and assets. This must be conducted with an understanding of the enterprise's present and future attitude toward risk and IT risk position.

Before creating the Current Profile, the implementer should review the Framework Implementation Tiers as described in **figure 13**. Selection of the appropriate Tier that will attain stakeholder needs in an optimal way will establish the scale for answering the question, "Where are we now?" The goal of the process is to establish the appropriate levels of governance and management to accomplish the risk objectives defined in phase 1. Selection of a Tier that is less than suitable may result in the lack of sufficient processes to address risk or to coordinate with other entities. Improper selection of the highest Tier, however, may impose costly organizationwide programs and processes whose benefits are not commensurate with the phase 1 goals defined. The dialogue to determine appropriate goals, Tiers and activities, in consideration of the unique organizational context, is one of the key benefits of applying the CSF.

The CSF Version 1.0 Core contains approximately 100 subcategories of outcomes, many of which are supported by one or more COBIT process. For the CSF, the user should create the Current Profile for all of the subcategories. Viewed through the lens of the organizational tier, which helps inform *how* an outcome should be accomplished, the implementer iterates through each subcategory and determines the level to which that outcome has been attained to fulfill stakeholder goals. For each row in the template, determine and record the current level of achievement, as guided by the principles in the COBIT PAM and in *COBIT® Assessor's Guide: Using COBIT® 5*. The assessor guide provides detailed criteria for determining appropriate activities to achieve the outcomes. In consideration of that guidance, select the appropriate level of achievement for each subcategory according to the scale detailed in **figure 17**.

Figure 17—Achievement Rating Scale		
Abbreviation	**Description**	**% Achieved**
N	Not achieved	0 to 15
P	Partially achieved	>15 to 50
L	Largely achieved	>50 to 85
F	Fully achieved	>85 to 100
Source: This figure is adapted from ISO 15504-2:2003, Section 5.7.2, on pages 10-11, with the permission of ANSI on behalf of ISO. © ISO 2014 - All rights reserved.		

Appendix B provides a full COBIT Current Profile template based on the CSF Core, including a detailed description of the Current Profile elements in **figure B.2**.

Implementation Considerations
Purpose
To gain an understanding of the organizational systems and assets that enable the mission described in phase 1, determining specific IT goals for protecting those systems [in accordance with business impact requirements] To understand overarching threats to, and vulnerabilities of, those systems and assets, and use the Current Profile template to record current outcome achievement levels
Inputs
• Organizational mission and drivers • Understanding of the cascading goals • Statement of how business and IT function deliver value from IT • Understanding of the enterprise's present and future attitude toward risk and IT risk position • Framework Implementation Tiers

Implementation Considerations *(cont.)*
High-level Activities
• Determine business and operational systems on which stakeholder drivers (as described in phase 1) depend. Determination should include any downstream dependencies for identified systems and assets.   • Ascertain availability goals and/or recovery goals for identified systems and assets in order to provide stakeholder value and fulfill organizational obligations (e.g., contractual availability requirements, critical infrastructure service requirements, service level agreements).   • Review the Framework Implementation Tiers and record the Tier selected for the organization (within the scope determined in phase 1).   • Considering the characteristics of the desired Tier, using the COBIT 5 assessment methodology (based on ISO 15504), complete the Current Profile template, iterating through each subcategory and recording current status ranging from Not Achieved to Fully Achieved. Ensure that appropriate rationale/evidence is included for each component.
Outputs
• Threats to, and vulnerabilities of, important systems and assets   • Organizational risk assessment   • Current Profile   • IT-enabled service catalog   • Service agreements   • Availability, performance and capacity baselines for future comparison

Relevant COBIT 5 Practices	
COBIT 5 Practice	**Description**
APO02.01	Understand enterprise direction. Consider the current enterprise environment and business processes, as well as the enterprise strategy and future objectives. Consider also the external environment of the enterprise (industry drivers, relevant regulations, basis for competition).
APO02.02	Assess the current environment, capabilities and performance. Assess the performance of current internal business and IT capabilities and external IT services, and develop an understanding of the enterprise architecture in relation to IT. Identify issues currently being experienced and develop recommendations in areas that could benefit from improvement. Consider service provider differentiators and options and the financial impact and potential costs and benefits of using external services.
APO03.02	Define reference architecture. The reference architecture describes the current and target architectures for the business, information, data, application and technology domains.
APO04.01	Create an environment conducive to innovation. Create an environment that is conducive to innovation, considering issues such as culture, reward, collaboration, technology forums, and mechanisms to promote and capture employee ideas.
APO07.02	Identify key IT personnel. Identify key IT personnel while minimizing reliance on a single individual performing a critical job function through knowledge capture (documentation), knowledge sharing, succession planning and staff backup.

Relevant COBIT 5 Practices *(cont.)*	
COBIT 5 Practice	**Description**
APO07.03	Maintain the skills and competencies of personnel. Define and manage the skills and competencies required of personnel. Regularly verify that personnel have the competencies to fulfill their roles on the basis of their education, training and/or experience, and verify that these competencies are being maintained, using qualification and certification programs where appropriate. Provide employees with ongoing learning and opportunities to maintain their knowledge, skills and competencies at a level required to achieve enterprise goals.
APO07.05	Plan and track the usage of IT and business human resources. Understand and track the current and future demand for business and IT human resources with responsibilities for enterprise IT. Identify shortfalls and provide input into sourcing plans, enterprise and IT recruitment processes sourcing plans, and business and IT recruitment processes.
APO09.01	Identify IT services. Analyze business requirements and the way in which IT-enabled services and service levels support business processes. Discuss and agree on potential services and service levels with the business, and compare them with the current service portfolio to identify new or changed services or service level options.
APO09.02	Catalog IT-enabled services. Define and maintain one or more service catalogues for relevant target groups. Publish and maintain live IT-enabled services in the service catalogues.
APO09.03	Define and prepare service agreements. Define and prepare service agreements based on the options in the service catalogues. Include internal operational agreements.
APO11.02	Define and manage quality standards, practices and procedures. Identify and maintain requirements, standards, procedures and practices for key processes to guide the enterprise in meeting the intent of the agreed-on QMS. This should be in line with the IT control framework requirements. Consider certification for key processes, organizational units, products or services.
APO12.01	Collect data. Identify and collect relevant data to enable effective IT-related risk identification, analysis and reporting.
BAI03.11	Define IT services and maintain the service portfolio. Define and agree on new or changed IT services and service level options. Document new or changed service definitions and service level options to be updated in the services portfolio.
BAI04.01	Assess current availability, performance and capacity and create a baseline. Assess availability, performance and capacity of services and resources to ensure that cost-justifiable capacity and performance are available to support business needs and deliver against SLAs. Create availability, performance and capacity baselines for future comparison.
BAI04.03	Plan for new or changed service requirements. Plan and prioritize availability, performance and capacity implications of changing business needs and service requirements.
BAI09.01	Identify and record current assets. Maintain an up-to-date and accurate record of all IT assets required to deliver services and ensure alignment with configuration management and financial management.

Relevant COBIT 5 Practices *(cont.)*	
COBIT 5 Practice	**Description**
BAI09.02	Manage critical assets. Identify assets that are critical in providing service capability and take steps to maximize their reliability and availability to support business needs.
BAI10.01	Establish and maintain a configuration model. Establish and maintain a logical model of the services, assets and infrastructure and how to record configuration items (CIs) and the relationships among them. Include the CIs considered necessary to manage services effectively and to provide a single reliable description of the assets in a service.
BAI10.02	Establish and maintain a configuration repository and baseline. Establish and maintain a configuration management repository and create controlled configuration baselines.
BAI10.03	Maintain and control configuration items. Maintain an up-to-date repository of configuration items by populating with changes.
MEA03.01	Identify external compliance requirements. On a continuous basis, identify and monitor for changes in local and international laws, regulations and other external requirements that must be complied with from an IT perspective.
MEA03.02	Optimize response to external requirements. Review and adjust policies, principles, standards, procedures and methodologies to ensure that legal, regulatory and contractual requirements are addressed and communicated. Consider industry standards, codes of good practice and good practice guidance for adoption and adaptation.

CSF Step 4: Conduct a Risk Assessment, and Step 5: Create a Target Profile
COBIT Phase 3—Where Do We Want To Be?

Based on the assessed Current Profile process capability levels, and using the results of the goals analysis/process identification performed earlier, an appropriate target capability level should be determined for each process. The chosen level should consider any relevant external and internal benchmarks (e.g., government-provided templates or guidance). With the understanding of vulnerabilities and threats to valuable assets, as determined in phase 2, perform a comprehensive risk assessment to determine how best to protect those assets, detect and respond to attacks on them, and recover from any degradation or interruption. In *COBIT 5 for Risk*, appendix C titled Core COBIT 5 Risk Management Processes provides a comprehensive approach to identify, assess and reduce IT-related risk within levels of tolerance set by enterprise executive management.

Note that CSF Steps 3 and 5 may be reversed,
depending on organizational preference.

The result (Step 6) is expected to remain the same whether the reader:
1) Decides where to go, where is here, then how to get there from here; or,
2) Decides where is here, where to go, then how to get from here to there.

Viewed through the lens of the organizational tier, which helps inform how an outcome should be accomplished, iterate through each of the subcategories and determine the level to which that outcome should be attained in a manner that fulfills enterprise goals. For each row in the template, determine and record the target level of achievement as guided by the principles in the COBIT PAM and in *COBIT Assessor's Guide: Using COBIT® 5*. The assessor guide provides detailed criteria for determining the appropriate activities to achieve the outcomes. In consideration of that guidance, select the appropriate level of achievement for each subcategory according to the scale shown in **figure 18**.

Figure 18—Achievement Rating Scale		
Abbreviation	**Description**	**% Achieved**
N	Not achieved	0 to 15
P	Partially achieved	>15 to 50
L	Largely achieved	>50 to 85
F	Fully achieved	>85 to 100
Source: This figure is adapted from ISO 15504-2:2003, Section 5.7.2, on pages 10-11, with the permission of ANSI on behalf of ISO. © ISO 2014 - All rights reserved.		

Appendix B provides a full COBIT Target Profile template based on the CSF Core, including a detailed description of the Target Profile elements in **figure B.3**.

Implementation Considerations
Purpose
To gain an understanding of the security-specific goals, for organizational systems and assets that enable the mission described in phase 1, to attain stakeholder risk management goals Having identified overarching threats to, and vulnerabilities of, those systems and assets, to discern the likelihood of a cybersecurity event and the potential organization impact.
Inputs
• Current Profile • Process capability levels/Framework Implementation Tiers • Results of goals analysis/process identification • Security-related goals for applicable systems and assets

Implementation Considerations *(cont.)*

High-level Activities

- Based on recorded security-related goals for applicable systems and assets, conduct risk analysis activities to catalog potential security risk events to those systems and assets.
- For each potential event recorded above, determine the likelihood of that potential being realized and the potential impact on the organization. The CSF notes that it is important that organizations seek to incorporate emerging risk, threat and vulnerability data to facilitate a robust understanding of the likelihood and impact of cybersecurity events.
- Determine whether any Framework Core subcategories are Not Applicable to the systems and assets identified as the scope as an output from phase 1.
- Determine whether additional categories/subcategories (as security-specific goals) should be added to the Target Profile to account for unique organizational risk.
- Considering the characteristics of the desired Tier (as determined in phase 2 and recorded in the Current Profile), using the COBIT 5 assessment methodology (based on ISO 15504), complete the Target Profile template, iterating through each subcategory and recording desired state ranging from Not Achieved to Fully Achieved. Note that Fully Achieved may not necessarily be the desirable state, and that subcategory outcomes may not need to be achieved to the highest Tier description. Ensure that appropriate rationale/evidence is included for each component.

Outputs

- Catalog potential security risk events to critical systems and assets
- Target capability level
- Comprehensive risk assessment
- Target Profile
- Business impact assessment results
- Reference architecture

Relevant COBIT 5 Practices	
COBIT 5 Practice	**Description**
APO02.03	Define the target IT capabilities. Define the target business and IT capabilities and required IT services. This should be based on the understanding of the enterprise environment and requirements; the assessment of the current business process and IT environment and issues; and consideration of reference standards, good practices and validated emerging technologies or innovation proposals.
APO03.02	Define reference architecture. The reference architecture describes the current and target architectures for the business, information, data, application and technology domains.
APO04.01	Create an environment conducive to innovation. Create an environment that is conducive to innovation, considering issues such as culture, reward, collaboration, technology forums, and mechanisms to promote and capture employee ideas.
APO07.02	Identify key IT personnel. Identify key IT personnel while minimizing reliance on a single individual performing a critical job function through knowledge capture (documentation), knowledge sharing, succession planning and staff backup.

Relevant COBIT 5 Practices *(cont.)*	
COBIT 5 Practice	**Description**
APO07.03	Maintain the skills and competencies of personnel. Define and manage the skills and competencies required of personnel. Regularly verify that personnel have the competencies to fulfill their roles on the basis of their education, training and/or experience, and verify that these competencies are being maintained, using qualification and certification programs where appropriate. Provide employees with ongoing learning and opportunities to maintain their knowledge, skills and competencies at a level required to achieve enterprise goals.
APO07.05	Plan and track the usage of IT and business human resources. Understand and track the current and future demand for business and IT human resources with responsibilities for enterprise IT. Identify shortfalls and provide input into sourcing plans, enterprise and IT recruitment processes sourcing plans, and business and IT recruitment processes.
APO09.01	Identify IT services. Analyze business requirements and the way in which IT-enabled services and service levels support business processes. Discuss and agree on potential services and service levels with the business, and compare them with the current service portfolio to identify new or changed services or service level options.
APO09.02	Catalog IT-enabled services. Define and maintain one or more service catalogues for relevant target groups. Publish and maintain live IT-enabled services in the service catalogues.
APO09.03	Define and prepare service agreements. Define and prepare service agreements based on the options in the service catalogues. Include internal operational agreements.
APO11.02	Define and manage quality standards, practices and procedures. Identify and maintain requirements, standards, procedures and practices for key processes to guide the enterprise in meeting the intent of the agreed-on QMS. This should be in line with the IT control framework requirements. Consider certification for key processes, organizational units, products or services.
APO12.01	Collect data. Identify and collect relevant data to enable effective IT-related risk identification, analysis and reporting.
BAI03.11	Define IT services and maintain the service portfolio. Define and agree on new or changed IT services and service level options. Document new or changed service definitions and service level options to be updated in the services portfolio.
BAI04.01	Assess current availability, performance and capacity and create a baseline. Assess availability, performance and capacity of services and resources to ensure that cost-justifiable capacity and performance are available to support business needs and deliver against SLAs. Create availability, performance and capacity baselines for future comparison.
BAI04.03	Plan for new or changed service requirements. Plan and prioritize availability, performance and capacity implications of changing business needs and service requirements.
BAI09.01	Identify and record current assets. Maintain an up-to-date and accurate record of all IT assets required to deliver services and ensure alignment with configuration management and financial management.

COBIT 5 Practice	Description
Relevant COBIT 5 Practices (cont.)	
BAI09.02	Manage critical assets. Identify assets that are critical in providing service capability and take steps to maximize their reliability and availability to support business needs.
BAI10.01	Establish and maintain a configuration model. Establish and maintain a logical model of the services, assets and infrastructure and how to record configuration items (CIs) and the relationships amongst them. Include the CIs considered necessary to manage services effectively and to provide a single reliable description of the assets in a service.
BAI10.02	Establish and maintain a configuration repository and baseline. Establish and maintain a configuration management repository and create controlled configuration baselines.
BAI10.03	Maintain and control configuration items. Maintain an up-to-date repository of configuration items by populating with changes.
DSS06 (all)	Define and maintain appropriate business process controls to ensure that information related to and processed by in-house or outsourced business processes satisfies all relevant information control requirements. Identify the relevant information control requirements and manage and operate adequate controls to ensure that information and information processing satisfy these requirements.
MEA03.01	Identify external compliance requirements. On a continuous basis, identify and monitor for changes in local and international laws, regulations and other external requirements that must be complied with from an IT perspective.
MEA03.02	Optimize response to external requirements. Review and adjust policies, principles, standards, procedures and methodologies to ensure that legal, regulatory and contractual requirements are addressed and communicated. Consider industry standards, codes of good practice, and good practice guidance for adoption and adaptation.

CSF Step 6: Determine, Analyze, and Prioritize Gaps.
COBIT Phase 4—What Needs To Be Done?

For each of the subcategories in the Target Profile, consider the difference between the target level of achievement and the current level. The result of this gap assessment will help identify organizational strengths and weaknesses. *COBIT 5 Implementation* highlights several important considerations for this phase:

> *This phase may identify some relatively easy-to-achieve improvements such as improved training, the sharing of good practices and standardizing procedures; however, the gap analysis is likely to require considerable experience in business and IT management techniques to develop practical solutions. Experience in undertaking behavioral and organizational change will also be needed.*

> *Understanding of process techniques, advanced business and technical expertise, and knowledge of business and system management software applications and services may be needed. To ensure that this phase is executed effectively, it is important for the team to work with the business*

and IT process owners and other required stakeholders, engaging internal expertise. If necessary, external advice should also be obtained. Risk that will not be mitigated after closing the gaps should be identified and, if acceptable, formally accepted by management.

The opportunities for improvement should be documented in a prioritized action plan to address gaps. The plan should draw on mission drivers, a cost/benefit analysis, and understanding of impact and likelihood of risk to achieve the outcomes as described in the Target Profile. The plan should also include consideration of the resources necessary to address the gaps. Using Profiles in this manner enables the organization to make informed decisions about cybersecurity activities; supports risk management; and enables the organization to perform cost-effective, targeted improvements.

Implementation Considerations
Purpose
To understand what actions are required to attain stakeholder goals through identification of gaps between the current and target environments and alignment with organizational priorities and resources
Inputs
• Target Profile • Process, business and technical expertise • Resource requirements
High-level Activities
• For each subcategory listed in the Target Profile, record the difference between the desired capability level and the current state (as recorded in the Current Profile), if any. • For each subcategory where a difference between Current and Target state was recorded, utilizing *COBIT 5: Enabling Processes* (as included in the Framework Core), determine required activities and detailed activities. These are described in *COBIT 5: Enabling Processes* as the how, why and what to implement for each governance or management practice to improve IT performance and/or address IT solution and service delivery risk. Additional informative references from the Framework Core may assist with determining appropriate controls or activities. • Reviewing the potential activities defined, determine the appropriate priority of those activities to enable optimal value realization while providing reasonable assurance that risk management practices are appropriate to ensure that the actual IT risk does not exceed agreed-on risk appetite. • Determine the resources necessary to accomplish the activities described, in consideration of stakeholder guidance from phase 1 regarding available resources. • Create and record an action plan of activities with milestones, ensuring appropriate responsibility and accountability, to achieve the desired outcomes according to the determined priorities.
Outputs
• Profile gap assessment • Prioritized action plan • Risk acceptance documentation • Performance and conformance targets

Relevant COBIT 5 Practices	
COBIT 5 Practice	Description
EDM01.02	Direct the governance system. Inform leaders and obtain their support, buy-in and commitment. Guide the structures, processes and practices for the governance of IT in line with agreed-on governance design principles, decision-making models and authority levels. Define the information required for informed decision making.
EDM02.02	Direct value optimization. Direct value management principles and practices to enable optimal value realization from IT-enabled investments throughout their full economic life cycle.
EDM03.02	Direct risk management. Direct the establishment of risk management practices to provide reasonable assurance that IT risk management practices are appropriate to ensure that the actual IT risk does not exceed the board's risk appetite.
EDM04.02	Direct resource management. Ensure the adoption of resource management principles to enable optimal use of IT resources throughout their full economic life cycle.
EDM05.02	Direct stakeholder communication and reporting. Ensure the establishment of effective stakeholder communication and reporting, including mechanisms for ensuring the quality and completeness of information, oversight of mandatory reporting, and creating a communication strategy for stakeholders.
APO02.05	Define the strategic plan and road map. Create a strategic plan that defines, in co-operation with relevant stakeholders, how IT-related goals will contribute to the enterprise's strategic goals. Include how IT will support IT-enabled investment programs, business processes, IT services and IT assets. Direct IT to define the initiatives that will be required to close the gaps, the sourcing strategy and the measurements to be used to monitor achievement of goals, then prioritize the initiatives and combine them in a high-level road map.
APO02.06	Communicate the IT strategy and direction. Create awareness and understanding of the business and IT objectives and direction, as captured in the IT strategy, through communication to appropriate stakeholders and users throughout the enterprise.
APO08.04	Co-ordinate and communicate. Work with stakeholders and co-ordinate the end-to-end delivery of IT services and solutions provided to the business.
APO11.05	Integrate quality management into solutions for development and service delivery. Incorporate relevant quality management practices into the definition, monitoring, reporting and ongoing management of solutions development and service offerings.
BAI02.04	Obtain approval of requirements and solutions. Co-ordinate feedback from affected stakeholders and, at predetermined key stages, obtain business sponsor or product owner approval and sign-off on functional and technical requirements, feasibility studies, risk analyses and recommended solutions.
BAI03.01	Design high-level solutions. Develop and document high-level designs using agreed-on and appropriate phased or rapid agile development techniques. Ensure alignment with the IT strategy and enterprise architecture. Reassess and update the designs when significant issues occur during detailed design or building phases or as the solution evolves. Ensure that stakeholders actively participate in the design and approve each version.

Relevant COBIT 5 Practices *(cont.)*	
COBIT 5 Practice	Description
BAI03.02	Design detailed solution components. Develop, document and elaborate detailed designs progressively using agreed-on and appropriate phased or rapid agile development techniques, addressing all components (business processes and related automated and manual controls, supporting IT applications, infrastructure services and technology products, and partners/suppliers). Ensure that the detailed design includes internal and external service level agreements (SLAs) and operating level agreements (OLAs).
BAI03.03	Develop solution components. Develop solution components progressively in accordance with detailed designs following development methods and documentation standards, quality assurance (QA) requirements, and approval standards. Ensure that all control requirements in the business processes, supporting IT applications and infrastructure services, services and technology products, and partners/suppliers are addressed.
BAI03.04	Procure solution components. Procure solution components based on the acquisition plan in accordance with requirements and detailed designs, architecture principles and standards, and the enterprise's overall procurement and contract procedures, QA requirements, and approval standards. Ensure that all legal and contractual requirements are identified and addressed by the supplier.
BAI03.05	Build solutions. Install and configure solutions and integrate with business process activities. Implement control, security and auditability measures during configuration, and during integration of hardware and infrastructural software, to protect resources and ensure availability and data integrity. Update the services catalogue to reflect the new solutions.
BAI03.06	Perform QA. Develop, resource and execute a QA plan aligned with the QMS to obtain the quality specified in the requirements definition and the enterprise's quality policies and procedures.
BAI03.07	Prepare for solution testing. Establish a test plan and required environments to test the individual and integrated solution components, including the business processes and supporting services, applications and infrastructure.
BAI03.08	Execute solution testing. Execute testing continually during development, including control testing, in accordance with the defined test plan and development practices in the appropriate environment. Engage business process owners and end users in the test team. Identify, log and prioritize errors and issues identified during testing.
BAI05.01	Establish the desire to change. Understand the scope and impact of the envisioned change and stakeholder readiness/willingness to change. Identify actions to motivate stakeholders to accept and want to make the change work successfully.
BAI05.02	Form an effective implementation team. Establish an effective implementation team by assembling appropriate members, creating trust, and establishing common goals and effectiveness measures.
BAI05.03	Communicate desired vision. Communicate the desired vision for the change in the language of those affected by it. The communication should be made by senior management and include the rationale for, and benefits of, the change, the impacts of not making the change; and the vision, the road map and the involvement required of the various stakeholders.

Relevant COBIT 5 Practices *(cont.)*	
COBIT 5 Practice	Description
BAI05.04	Empower role players and identify short-term wins. Empower those with implementation roles by ensuring that accountabilities are assigned, providing training, and aligning organizational structures and human resources (HR) processes. Identify and communicate short-term wins that can be realized and are important from a change enablement perspective.
BAI05.05	Enable operation and use. Plan and implement all technical, operational and usage aspects such that all those who are involved in the future state environment can exercise their responsibility.
BAI05.06	Embed new approaches. Embed the new approaches by tracking implemented changes, assessing the effectiveness of the operation and use plan, and sustaining ongoing awareness through regular communication. Take corrective measures as appropriate, which may include enforcing compliance.
MEA01.01	Establish a monitoring approach. Engage with stakeholders to establish and maintain a monitoring approach to define the objectives, scope and method for measuring business solution and service delivery and contribution to enterprise objectives. Integrate this approach with the corporate performance management system.
MEA01.02	Set performance and conformance targets. Work with stakeholders to define, periodically review, update and approve performance and conformance targets within the performance measurement system.

CSF Step 7: Implement Action Plan
COBIT Phase 5—How Do We Get There?

Phase 5 includes the actual execution of the prioritized action plan, as defined in phase 4. Action plan execution provides an opportunity for frequent stakeholder communications, which should use language and terminology appropriate for each audience. For example, IT management discussions may consider specific facilities and processes, while board and executive discussions may be more related to annualized loss expectancy or market opportunities.

Action plan execution may be gradually implemented, building on the momentum of project success, building further credibility and improving success. The execution of the action plan provides an opportunity to foster an effective risk management culture throughout the organization. Performance measures and incremental metrics will help document success and support any adjustments required. Many such measures are described in the COBIT 5 processes, especially those in the Build, Acquire and Implement (BAI) and Deliver, Service and Support (DSS) domains.

Implementation Considerations
Purpose
To execute the plan, as defined in phase 4, to address gaps and improve security to achieve stakeholder goals in a prioritized and cost-effective manner
Inputs
• Prioritized action plan • Organizational mission and drivers • Performance and conformance targets
High-level Activities

• Execute the action plan as defined in phase 4. Consider root causes and success factors from the challenges listed in the COBIT 5 implementation guide including:
  – Make small improvements to test the approach and make sure it works.
  – Involve the process owners and other stakeholders in development of the improvement.
  – Apply adequate training where required.
  – Develop processes before attempting to automate.
  – Reorganize, if required, to enable better ownership of processes.
  – Match roles (specifically those that are key for successful adoption) to individual capabilities and characteristics.
  – Set clear, measurable and realistic goals (outcome expected from the improvement).
  – Set practical performance metrics (to monitor whether the improvement is driving achievement of goals).
  – Produce scorecards showing how performance is being measured.
  – Communicate in business impact terms the results and benefits being gained.
  – Implement quick wins and deliver solutions in short time scales.
  – Assess performance in meeting the original objectives and confirm realization of desired outcomes.
• Consider the need to redirect future activities and take corrective action.
• Assist in the resolution of significant issues, if required.
• If necessary, return to phase 3 and adjust Target Profile, Gap Assessment and Action Plan.

Outputs
• Operating procedures for implemented action items • Performance communications reports • Performance metrics results

Relevant COBIT 5 Practices	
COBIT 5 Practice	**Description**
EDM01.02	Direct the governance system. Inform leaders and obtain their support, buy-in and commitment. Guide the structures, processes and practices for the governance of IT in line with agreed-on governance design principles, decision-making models and authority levels. Define the information required for informed decision making.
EDM02.02	Direct value optimization. Direct value management principles and practices to enable optimal value realization from IT-enabled investments throughout their full economic life cycle.

Relevant COBIT 5 Practices *(cont.)*	
COBIT 5 Practice	**Description**
EDM03.02	Direct risk management. Direct the establishment of risk management practices to provide reasonable assurance that IT risk management practices are appropriate to ensure that the actual IT risk does not exceed the board's risk appetite.
EDM04.02	Direct resource management. Ensure the adoption of resource management principles to enable optimal use of IT resources throughout their full economic life cycle.
EDM05.02	Direct stakeholder communication and reporting. Ensure the establishment of effective stakeholder communication and reporting, including mechanisms for ensuring the quality and completeness of information, oversight of mandatory reporting, and creating a communication strategy for stakeholders.
APO02.05	Define the strategic plan and road map. Create a strategic plan that defines, in co-operation with relevant stakeholders, how IT-related goals will contribute to the enterprise's strategic goals. Include how IT will support IT-enabled investment programs, business processes, IT services and IT assets. Direct IT to define the initiatives that will be required to close the gaps, the sourcing strategy and the measurements to be used to monitor achievement of goals, then prioritize the initiatives and combine them in a high-level road map.
APO02.06	Communicate the IT strategy and direction. Create awareness and understanding of the business and IT objectives and direction, as captured in the IT strategy, through communication to appropriate stakeholders and users throughout the enterprise.
APO08.04	Co-ordinate and communicate. Work with stakeholders and co-ordinate the end-to-end delivery of IT services and solutions provided to the business.
APO11.05	Integrate quality management into solutions for development and service delivery. Incorporate relevant quality management practices into the definition, monitoring, reporting and ongoing management of solutions development and service offerings.
BAI02.04	Obtain approval of requirements and solutions. Co-ordinate feedback from affected stakeholders and, at predetermined key stages, obtain business sponsor or product owner approval and sign-off on functional and technical requirements, feasibility studies, risk analyses and recommended solutions.
BAI03.01	Design high-level solutions. Develop and document high-level designs using agreed-on and appropriate phased or rapid agile development techniques. Ensure alignment with the IT strategy and enterprise architecture. Reassess and update the designs when significant issues occur during detailed design or building phases or as the solution evolves. Ensure that stakeholders actively participate in the design and approve each version.
BAI03.02	Design detailed solution components. Develop, document and elaborate detailed designs progressively using agreed-on and appropriate phased or rapid agile development techniques, addressing all components (business processes and related automated and manual controls, supporting IT applications, infrastructure services and technology products, and partners/suppliers). Ensure that the detailed design includes internal and external SLAs and OLAs.

Relevant COBIT 5 Practices *(cont.)*	
COBIT 5 Practice	**Description**
BAI03.03	Develop solution components. Develop solution components progressively in accordance with detailed designs following development methods and documentation standards, QA requirements, and approval standards. Ensure that all control requirements in the business processes, supporting IT applications and infrastructure services, services and technology products, and partners/suppliers are addressed.
BAI03.04	Procure solution components. Procure solution components based on the acquisition plan in accordance with requirements and detailed designs, architecture principles and standards, and the enterprise's overall procurement and contract procedures, QA requirements, and approval standards. Ensure that all legal and contractual requirements are identified and addressed by the supplier.
BAI03.05	Build solutions. Install and configure solutions and integrate with business process activities. Implement control, security and auditability measures during configuration, and during integration of hardware and infrastructural software, to protect resources and ensure availability and data integrity. Update the services catalogue to reflect the new solutions.
BAI03.06	Perform QA. Develop, resource and execute a QA plan aligned with the QMS to obtain the quality specified in the requirements definition and the enterprise's quality policies and procedures.
BAI03.07	Prepare for solution testing. Establish a test plan and required environments to test the individual and integrated solution components, including the business processes and supporting services, applications and infrastructure.
BAI03.08	Execute solution testing. Execute testing continually during development, including control testing, in accordance with the defined test plan and development practices in the appropriate environment. Engage business process owners and end users in the test team. Identify, log and prioritize errors and issues identified during testing.
BAI05.01	Establish the desire to change. Understand the scope and impact of the envisioned change and stakeholder readiness/willingness to change. Identify actions to motivate stakeholders to accept and want to make the change work successfully.
BAI05.02	Form an effective implementation team. Establish an effective implementation team by assembling appropriate members, creating trust, and establishing common goals and effectiveness measures.
BAI05.03	Communicate desired vision. Communicate the desired vision for the change in the language of those affected by it. The communication should be made by senior management and include the rationale for, and benefits of, the change, the impacts of not making the change; and the vision, the road map and the involvement required of the various stakeholders.
BAI05.04	Empower role players and identify short-term wins. Empower those with implementation roles by ensuring that accountabilities are assigned, providing training, and aligning organizational structures and HR processes. Identify and communicate short-term wins that can be realized and are important from a change enablement perspective.

Relevant COBIT 5 Practices *(cont.)*	
COBIT 5 Practice	**Description**
BAI05.05	Enable operation and use. Plan and implement all technical, operational and usage aspects such that all those who are involved in the future state environment can exercise their responsibility.
BAI05.06	Embed new approaches. Embed the new approaches by tracking implemented changes, assessing the effectiveness of the operation and use plan, and sustaining ongoing awareness through regular communication. Take corrective measures as appropriate, which may include enforcing compliance.
MEA01.01	Establish a monitoring approach. Engage with stakeholders to establish and maintain a monitoring approach to define the objectives, scope and method for measuring business solution and service delivery and contribution to enterprise objectives. Integrate this approach with the corporate performance management system.
MEA01.02	Set performance and conformance targets. Work with stakeholders to define, periodically review, update and approve performance and conformance targets within the performance measurement system.
MEA01.03	Collect and process performance and conformance data. Collect and process timely and accurate data aligned with enterprise approaches.
DSS01.01	Perform operational procedures. Maintain and perform operational procedures and operational tasks reliably and consistently.
DSS01.02	Manage outsourced IT services. Manage the operation of outsourced IT services to maintain the protection of enterprise information and reliability of service delivery.
DSS01.04	Manage the environment. Maintain measures for protection against environmental factors. Install specialized equipment and devices to monitor and control the environment.
DSS01.05	Manage facilities. Manage facilities, including power and communications equipment, in line with laws and regulations, technical and business requirements, vendor specifications, and health and safety guidelines.
DSS02.02	Record, classify and prioritize requests and incidents. Identify, record and classify service requests and incidents, and assign a priority according to business criticality and service agreements.
DSS02.03	Verify, approve and fulfill service requests. Select the appropriate request procedures and verify that the service requests fulfill defined request criteria. Obtain approval, if required, and fulfill the requests.
DSS02.04	Investigate, diagnose and allocate incidents. Identify and record incident symptoms, determine possible causes, and allocate for resolution.
DSS02.05	Resolve and recover from incidents. Document, apply and test the identified solutions or workarounds and perform recovery actions to restore the IT-related service.
DSS02.06	Close service requests and incidents. Verify satisfactory incident resolution and/or request fulfillment, and close.
DSS02.07	Track status and produce reports. Regularly track, analyze and report incident and request fulfillment trends to provide information for continual improvement.

Relevant COBIT 5 Practices *(cont.)*	
COBIT 5 Practice	**Description**
DSS03.01	Identify and classify problems. Define and implement criteria and procedures to report problems identified, including problem classification, categorization and prioritization.
DSS03.02	Investigate and diagnose problems. Investigate and diagnose problems using relevant subject management experts to assess and analyze root causes.
DSS03.03	Raise known errors. As soon as the root causes of problems are identified, create known-error records and an appropriate workaround, and identify potential solutions.
DSS03.04	Resolve and close problems. Identify and initiate sustainable solutions addressing the root cause, raising change requests via the established change management process if required to resolve errors. Ensure that the personnel affected are aware of the actions taken and the plans developed to prevent future incidents from occurring.
DSS03.05	Perform proactive problem management. Collect and analyze operational data (especially incident and change records) to identify emerging trends that may indicate problems. Log problem records to enable assessment.
DSS04.02	Maintain a continuity strategy. Evaluate business continuity management options and choose a cost-effective and viable continuity strategy that will ensure enterprise recovery and continuity in the face of a disaster or other major incident or disruption.
DSS04.03	Develop and implement a business continuity response. Develop a business continuity plan (BCP) based on the strategy that documents the procedures and information in readiness for use in an incident to enable the enterprise to continue its critical activities.
DSS04.04	Exercise, test and review the BCP. Test the continuity arrangements on a regular basis to exercise the recovery plans against predetermined outcomes and to allow innovative solutions to be developed and help to verify over time that the plan will work as anticipated.
DSS04.05	Review, maintain and improve the continuity plan. Conduct a management review of the continuity capability at regular intervals to ensure its continued suitability, adequacy and effectiveness. Manage changes to the plan in accordance with the change control process to ensure that the continuity plan is kept up to date and continually reflects actual business requirements.
DSS04.06	Conduct continuity plan training. Provide all concerned internal and external parties with regular training sessions regarding the procedures and their roles and responsibilities in case of disruption.
DSS04.07	Manage backup arrangements. Maintain availability of business-critical information.
DSS04.08	Conduct post-resumption review. Assess the adequacy of the BCP following the successful resumption of business processes and services after a disruption.
DSS05.01	Protect against malware. Implement and maintain preventive, detective and corrective measures in place (especially up-to-date security patches and virus control) across the enterprise to protect information systems and technology from malware (e.g., viruses, worms, spyware, spam).
DSS05.02	Manage network and connectivity security. Use security measures and related management procedures to protect information over all methods of connectivity.

Relevant COBIT 5 Practices *(cont.)*	
COBIT 5 Practice	**Description**
DSS05.03	Manage endpoint security. Ensure that endpoints (e.g., laptop, desktop, server, and other mobile and network devices or software) are secured at a level that is equal to or greater than the defined security requirements of the information processed, stored or transmitted.
DSS05.04	Manage user identity and logical access. Ensure that all users have information access rights in accordance with their business requirements and co-ordinate with business units that manage their own access rights within business processes.
DSS05.05	Manage physical access to IT assets. Define and implement procedures to grant, limit and revoke access to premises, buildings and areas according to business needs, including emergencies. Access to premises, buildings and areas should be justified, authorized, logged and monitored. This should apply to all persons entering the premises, including staff, temporary staff, clients, vendors, visitors or any other third party.
DSS05.06	Manage sensitive documents and output devices. Establish appropriate physical safeguards, accounting practices and inventory management over sensitive IT assets, such as special forms, negotiable instruments, special-purpose printers or security tokens.
DSS05.07	Monitor the infrastructure for security-related events. Using intrusion detection tools, monitor the infrastructure for unauthorized access and ensure that any events are integrated with general event monitoring and incident management.
DSS06.02	Control the processing of information. Operate the execution of the business process activities and related controls, based on enterprise risk, to ensure that information processing is valid, complete, accurate, timely, and secure (i.e., reflects legitimate and authorized business use).
DSS06.03	Manage roles, responsibilities, access privileges and levels of authority. Manage the business roles, responsibilities, levels of authority and segregation of duties needed to support the business process objectives. Authorize access to any information assets related to business information processes, including those under the custody of the business, IT and third parties. This ensures that the business knows where the data are and who is handling data on its behalf.
DSS06.04	Manage errors and exceptions. Manage business process exceptions and errors and facilitate their correction. Include escalation of business process errors and exceptions and the execution of defined corrective actions. This provides assurance of the accuracy and integrity of the business information process.
DSS06.05	Ensure traceability of Information events and accountabilities. Ensure that business information can be traced to the originating business event and accountable parties. This enables traceability of the information through its life cycle and related processes. This provides assurance that information that drives the business is reliable and has been processed in accordance with defined objectives.
DSS06.06	Secure information assets. Secure information assets accessible by the business through approved methods, including information in electronic form (such as methods that create new assets in any form, portable media devices, user applications and storage devices), information in physical form (such as source documents or output reports) and information during transit. This benefits the business by providing end-to-end safeguarding of information.

Relevant COBIT 5 Practices *(cont.)*	
COBIT 5 Practice	**Description**
MEA01.05	Ensure the implementation of corrective actions. Assist stakeholders in identifying, initiating and tracking corrective actions to address anomalies.
MEA02.02	Review business process controls effectiveness. Review the operation of controls, including a review of monitoring and test evidence, to ensure that controls within business processes operate effectively. Include activities to maintain evidence of the effective operation of controls through mechanisms such as periodic testing of controls, continuous controls monitoring, independent assessments, command and control centers, and network operations centers. This provides the business with the assurance of control effectiveness to meet requirements related to business, regulatory and social responsibilities.
MEA02.03	Perform control self-assessments. Encourage management and process owners to take positive ownership of control improvement through a continuing program of self-assessment to evaluate the completeness and effectiveness of management's control over processes, policies and contracts.
MEA02.04	Identify and report control deficiencies. Identify control deficiencies and analyze and identify their underlying root causes. Escalate control deficiencies and report to stakeholders.
MEA02.05	Ensure that assurance providers are independent and qualified. Ensure that the entities performing assurance are independent from the function, groups or organizations in scope. The entities performing assurance should demonstrate an appropriate attitude and appearance, competence in the skills and knowledge necessary to perform assurance, and adherence to codes of ethics and professional standards.
MEA02.06	Plan assurance initiatives. Plan assurance initiatives based on enterprise objectives and strategic priorities, inherent risk, resource constraints, and sufficient knowledge of the enterprise.
MEA02.08	Execute assurance initiatives. Execute the planned assurance initiative. Report on identified findings. Provide positive assurance opinions, where appropriate, and recommendations for improvement relating to identified operational performance, external compliance and internal control system residual risk.
MEA03.03	Confirm external compliance. Confirm compliance of policies, principles, standards, procedures and methodologies with legal, regulatory and contractual requirements.
MEA03.04	Obtain assurance of external compliance. Obtain and report assurance of compliance and adherence with policies, principles, standards, procedures and methodologies. Confirm that corrective actions to address compliance gaps are closed in a timely manner.

CSF Action Plan Review

COBIT Phase 6—Did We Get There?

Phase 6 provides the mechanisms to review the execution of the action plan and consider performance regarding the monitoring approach previously established (e.g., MEA01 processes from phases 4 and 5). Implementers should consider how well the organization achieved performance and conformance targets, updating ongoing improvement and communication activities in accordance with established change management processes. This review phase provides the opportunity to share both positive and negative results with stakeholders, fostering confidence in planned solutions and ensuring alignment with organizational drivers and goals.

Performance and conformance data may be shared with internal teams to improve subsequent processes. Appropriately sanitized risk, activity and performance results may be shared with external partners, consistent with the organizations' document classification policy for public documents, to help improve general understanding of IT risk management.

Implementation Considerations
Purpose
To review application of the improved governance and management practices and confirm that the action plan delivers the expected benefits
Inputs
• Operating procedures for implemented action items • Communications artifacts • Performance metrics • Action plan status reports
High-level Activities
• Assess the activities from phase 5 to assure that improvements and additions achieve the anticipated goals and attained risk management objectives. • Document lessons learned from implementation activities to improve future cycles and assist other organizations in similar exercises. • Identify any specific ongoing monitoring needs in support of phase 7.
Outputs
• Organizational assessment • Corrective action reports • Performance results to stakeholders • Lessons learned reports • Results information sharing

Relevant COBIT 5 Practices	
COBIT 5 Practice	**Description**
APO02.02	Assess the current environment, capabilities and performance. Assess the performance of current internal business and IT capabilities and external IT services, and develop an understanding of the enterprise architecture in relation to IT. Identify issues currently being experienced and develop recommendations in areas that could benefit from improvement. Consider service provider differentiators and options and the financial impact and potential costs and benefits of using external services.
MEA01.05	Ensure the implementation of corrective actions. Assist stakeholders in identifying, initiating and tracking corrective actions to address anomalies.

Relevant COBIT 5 Practices *(cont.)*	
COBIT 5 Practice	**Description**
MEA02.02	Review business process controls effectiveness. Review the operation of controls, including a review of monitoring and test evidence, to ensure that controls within business processes operate effectively. Include activities to maintain evidence of the effective operation of controls through mechanisms such as periodic testing of controls, continuous controls monitoring, independent assessments, command and control centers, and network operations centers. This provides the business with the assurance of control effectiveness to meet requirements related to business, regulatory and social responsibilities.
MEA02.03	Perform control self-assessments. Encourage management and process owners to take positive ownership of control improvement through a continuing program of self-assessment to evaluate the completeness and effectiveness of management's control over processes, policies and contracts.
MEA02.04	Identify and report control deficiencies. Identify control deficiencies and analyze and identify their underlying root causes. Escalate control deficiencies and report to stakeholders.
MEA02.05	Ensure that assurance providers are independent and qualified. Ensure that the entities performing assurance are independent from the function, groups or organizations in scope. The entities performing assurance should demonstrate an appropriate attitude and appearance, competence in the skills and knowledge necessary to perform assurance, and adherence to codes of ethics and professional standards.
MEA02.08	Execute assurance initiatives. Execute the planned assurance initiative. Report on identified findings. Provide positive assurance opinions, where appropriate, and recommendations for improvement relating to identified operational performance, external compliance and internal control system residual risk.
MEA03.04	Obtain assurance of external compliance. Obtain and report assurance of compliance and adherence with policies, principles, standards, procedures and methodologies. Confirm that corrective actions to address compliance gaps are closed in a timely manner.

CSF Life Cycle Management

COBIT Phase 7—How Do We Keep the Momentum Going?

An effective framework for GEIT addresses the complete life cycle of IT investment, ensuring that it creates value in alignment with enterprise objectives. Combining the CSF principles and COBIT 5 practices helps ensure value, managing risk and supporting mission drivers in accordance with the direction and support of the executive board and organizational business managers.

Phase 7 provides the opportunity to close the loop for communication workflow as introduced in chapter 2. As technical assessment is reported (e.g., through performance metrics such as those established through process MEA01) to business process owners, they, in turn, report progress toward enterprise goals and mission priorities, using language, approaches and communications that are meaningful to executive management. Momentum, gained by progress and effective communication, drives subsequent iterations of the life cycle. Updated challenges and opportunities lead to updated risk assessments and priorities, fostering organizational commitment and ownership of all accountabilities and responsibilities. In this way, successful governance and management processes become institutionalized in the culture.

Implementation Considerations
Purpose
To provide ongoing review/assessment of the overall success of the initiative, identify further governance or management requirements, and support continual improvement
Inputs
• Operating procedures • Monitoring plan • Performance metrics
High-level Activities
• Continually monitor the activities from phase 5 to assure that improvements and additions achieve the anticipated goals and attain risk management objectives. • Review effectiveness of improved governance and management practices and document benefits provided. • Document lessons learned from implementation activities to improve future cycles and assist other organizations in similar exercises.
Outputs
• Assurance of external compliance • Lessons learned reports • Performance results to stakeholders • Investment portfolio performance report(s) • Service level report(s) • Supplier performance and compliance report(s) • Customer satisfaction/QMS report(s) • Information security management system • Project performance reports against key project performance criteria • Change control plan(s) and results • Ongoing status and configuration reports

Relevant COBIT 5 Practices	
COBIT 5 Practice	**Description**
EDM01.03	Monitor the governance system. Monitor the effectiveness and performance of the enterprise's governance of IT. Assess whether the governance system and implemented mechanisms (including structures, principles and processes) are operating effectively and provide appropriate oversight of IT.
EDM02.01	Evaluate value optimization. Continually evaluate the portfolio of IT-enabled investments, services and assets to determine the likelihood of achieving enterprise objectives and delivering value at a reasonable cost. Identify and make judgment on any changes in direction that need to be given to management to optimize value creation.

COBIT 5 Practice	Description
Relevant COBIT 5 Practices *(cont.)*	
EDM02.03	Monitor value optimization. Monitor the key goals and metrics to determine the extent to which the business is generating the expected value and benefits to the enterprise from IT-enabled investments and services. Identify significant issues and consider corrective actions.
EDM03.03	Monitor risk management. Monitor the key goals and metrics of the risk management processes and establish how deviations or problems will be identified, tracked and reported for remediation.
EDM04.03	Monitor resource management. Monitor the key goals and metrics of the resource management processes and establish how deviations or problems will be identified, tracked and reported for remediation.
EDM05.03	Monitor stakeholder communication. Monitor the effectiveness of stakeholder communication. Assess mechanisms for ensuring accuracy, reliability and effectiveness, and ascertain whether the requirements of different stakeholders are met.
APO04.03	Monitor and scan the technology environment. Perform systematic monitoring and scanning of the enterprise's external environment to identify emerging technologies that have the potential to create value (e.g., by realizing the enterprise strategy, optimizing costs, avoiding obsolescence, and better enabling enterprise and IT processes). Monitor the marketplace, competitive landscape, industry sectors, and legal and regulatory trends to be able to analyze emerging technologies or innovation ideas in the enterprise context.
APO04.04	Assess the potential of emerging technologies and innovation ideas. Analyze identified emerging technologies and/or other IT innovation suggestions. Work with stakeholders to validate assumptions on the potential of new technologies and innovation.
APO04.05	Recommend appropriate further initiatives. Evaluate and monitor the results of proof-of-concept initiatives and, if favorable, generate recommendations for further initiatives and gain stakeholder support.
APO04.06	Monitor the implementation and use of innovation. Monitor the implementation and use of emerging technologies and innovations during integration, adoption and for the full economic life cycle to ensure that the promised benefits are realized and to identify lessons learned.
APO05.04	Monitor, optimize and report on investment portfolio performance. On a regular basis, monitor and optimize the performance of the investment portfolio and individual programs throughout the entire investment life cycle.
APO05.05	Maintain portfolios. Maintain portfolios of investment programs and projects, IT services and IT assets.
APO05.06	Manage benefits achievement. Monitor the benefits of providing and maintaining appropriate IT services and capabilities, based on the agreed-on and current business case.
APO07.05T	Track the usage of IT and business human resources. Track the current and future demand for business and IT human resources with responsibilities for enterprise IT. Identify shortfalls and provide input into sourcing plans, enterprise and IT recruitment processes sourcing plans, and business and IT recruitment processes.

Relevant COBIT 5 Practices *(cont.)*	
COBIT 5 Practice	**Description**
APO07.06	Manage contract staff. Ensure that consultants and contract personnel who support the enterprise with IT skills know and comply with the organization's policies and meet agreed-on contractual requirements.
APO08.05	Provide input to the continual improvement of services. Continually improve and evolve IT-enabled services and service delivery to the enterprise to align with changing enterprise and technology requirements.
APO09.04	Monitor and report service levels. Monitor service levels, report on achievements and identify trends. Provide the appropriate management information to aid performance management.
APO09.05	Review service agreements and contracts. Conduct periodic reviews of the service agreements and revise when needed.
APO10.03	Manage supplier relationships and contracts. Formalize and manage the supplier relationship for each supplier. Manage, maintain and monitor contracts and service delivery. Ensure that new or changed contracts conform to enterprise standards and legal and regulatory requirements. Deal with contractual disputes.
APO10.04	Manage supplier risk. Identify and manage risk relating to suppliers' ability to continually provide secure, efficient and effective service delivery.
APO10.05	Monitor supplier performance and compliance. Periodically review the overall performance of suppliers, compliance to contract requirements, and value for money, and address identified issues.
APO11.04	Perform quality monitoring, control and reviews. Monitor the quality of processes and services on an ongoing basis as defined by the QMS. Define, plan and implement measurements to monitor customer satisfaction with quality as well as the value the QMS provides. The information gathered should be used by the process owner to improve quality.
APO11.06	Maintain continuous improvement. Maintain and regularly communicate an overall quality plan that promotes continuous improvement. This should include the need for, and benefits of, continuous improvement. Collect and analyze data about the QMS, and improve its effectiveness. Correct non-conformities to prevent recurrence. Promote a culture of quality and continual improvement.
APO13.01	Establish and maintain an information security management system (ISMS). Establish and maintain an ISMS that provides a standard, formal and continuous approach to security management for information, enabling secure technology and business processes that are aligned with business requirements and enterprise security management.
APO13.02	Maintain an information security plan that describes how information security risk is to be managed and aligned with the enterprise strategy and enterprise architecture. Ensure that recommendations for implementing security improvements are based on approved business cases and implemented as an integral part of services and solutions development, then operated as an integral part of business operation.
APO13.03	Monitor and review the ISMS. Maintain and regularly communicate the need for, and benefits of, continuous information security improvement. Collect and analyze data about the ISMS, and improve the effectiveness of the ISMS. Correct non-conformities to prevent recurrence. Promote a culture of security and continual improvement.

Relevant COBIT 5 Practices *(cont.)*	
COBIT 5 Practice	**Description**
BAI01.06	Monitor, control and report on the program outcomes. Monitor and control program (solution delivery) and enterprise (value/outcome) performance against plan throughout the full economic life cycle of the investment. Report this performance to the program steering committee and the sponsors.
BAI01.10	Manage program and project risk. Eliminate or minimize specific risk associated with programs and projects through a systematic process of planning, identifying, analyzing, responding to, and monitoring and controlling the areas or events that have the potential to cause unwanted change. Risk faced by program and project management should be established and centrally recorded.
BAI01.11	Monitor and control projects. Measure project performance against key project performance criteria such as schedule, quality, cost and risk. Identify any deviations from the expected. Assess the impact of deviations on the project and overall program, and report results to key stakeholders.
BAI01.12	Manage project resources and work packages. Manage project work packages by placing formal requirements on authorizing and accepting work packages, and assigning and co-coordinating appropriate business and IT resources.
BAI03.09	Manage changes to requirements. Track the status of individual requirements (including all rejected requirements) throughout the project life cycle and manage the approval of changes to requirements.
BAI03.10	Maintain solutions. Develop and execute a plan for the maintenance of solution and infrastructure components. Include periodic reviews against business needs and operational requirements.
BAI04.04	Monitor and review availability and capacity. Monitor, measure, analyze, report and review availability, performance and capacity. Identify deviations from established baselines. Review trend analysis reports identifying any significant issues and variances, initiating actions where necessary, and ensuring that all outstanding issues are followed up.
BAI05.07	Sustain changes. Sustain changes through effective training of new staff, ongoing communication campaigns, continued top management commitment, adoption monitoring and sharing of lessons learned across the enterprise.
BAI06 (all)	Manage all changes in a controlled manner, including standard changes and emergency maintenance relating to business processes, applications and infrastructure. This includes change standards and procedures, impact assessment, prioritization and authorization, emergency changes, tracking, reporting, closure and documentation.
BAI07 (all)	Formally accept and make operational new solutions, including implementation planning, system and data conversion, acceptance testing, communication, release preparation, promotion to production of new or changed business processes and IT services, early production support, and a post-implementation review.
BAI08 (all)	Maintain the availability of relevant, current, validated and reliable knowledge to support all process activities and to facilitate decision making. Plan for the identification, gathering, organizing, maintaining, use and retirement of knowledge.
BAI10.03	Maintain and control configuration items. Maintain an up-to-date repository of configuration items by populating with changes.

Relevant COBIT 5 Practices *(cont.)*	
COBIT 5 Practice	**Description**
BAI10.04	Produce status and configuration reports. Define and produce configuration reports on status changes of configuration items.
BAI10.05	Verify and review integrity of the configuration repository. Periodically review the configuration repository and verify completeness and correctness against the desired target.
DSS01 (all)	Coordinate and execute the activities and operational procedures required to deliver internal and outsourced IT services, including the execution of pre-defined standard operating procedures and the required monitoring activities.
DSS02 (all)	Provide timely and effective response to user requests and resolution of all types of incidents. Restore normal service; record and fulfill user requests; and record, investigate, diagnose, escalate and resolve incidents.
DSS03 (all)	Identify and classify problems and their root causes and provide timely resolution to prevent recurring incidents. Provide recommendations for improvements.
DSS04 (all)	Establish and maintain a plan to enable the business and IT to respond to incidents and disruptions in order to continue operation of critical business processes and required IT services and maintain availability of information at a level acceptable to the enterprise.
MEA01.04	Analyze and report performance. Periodically review and report performance against targets, using a method that provides a succinct all-around view of IT performance and fits within the enterprise monitoring system.
MEA01.05	Ensure the implementation of corrective actions. Assist stakeholders in identifying, initiating and tracking corrective actions to address anomalies.
MEA02 (all)	Continuously monitor and evaluate the control environment, including self-assessments and independent assurance reviews. Enable management to identify control deficiencies and inefficiencies and to initiate improvement actions. Plan, organize and maintain standards for internal control assessment and assurance activities.

Page intentionally left blank

Chapter 4. Communicating Cybersecurity Requirements With Stakeholders

An important component of both the CSF and the COBIT 5 framework involves the governance and management of suppliers and business partners. A single business system may entail dozens of external stakeholders and supply chain/service providers. Each of these stakeholders brings opportunities to fulfill enterprise and IT-related goals; they also add additional vulnerability and potential risk to be considered. Implementation of the CSF using COBIT principles and processes provides a common language to communicate stakeholder needs and requirements.

The resulting process enables IT to be governed and managed in a holistic manner for the entire enterprise, supporting the primary organization as well as its supply chain partners, in applying an integrated framework. Many COBIT 5 practices include supplier components, guided by many elements of APO10 *Manage suppliers*. Specific examples of using the CSF through COBIT 5 with external business partners include:

• Document supplier management aspects. Cooperative agreements provide an opportunity to document the drivers, risk agreements and goals, using a subset of the processes in phase 1 (chapter 3).
• Record the result of supplier/partner assessments using the Current Profile template. Alignment around this CSF/COBIT model supports COBIT's principle of a single integrated framework model to record and communicate goals and performance.
• Record expectations and requirements through use of the Target Profile template described in chapter 3, phase 3. This model is helpful for conveying specific GEIT obligations, for example to a cloud provider to which the organization is exporting data.

Harmonization of processes and communications for both internal and external stakeholders improves consistency and simplifies tracking/reporting. Through use of common templates and communication practices, achievement of a holistic approach to governance and management of IT will ensure that goals are aligned and effective.

Page intentionally left blank

Appendix A: Framework Core

As described in chapter 2, the Framework Core provides a set of activities to achieve specific cybersecurity outcomes and references examples of guidance to achieve those outcomes. The Core is not a checklist of actions to perform. It presents key cybersecurity outcomes identified by industry as helpful in managing cybersecurity risk. The Core comprises four elements: Functions, Categories, Subcategories and Informative References.

The following table represents the Framework Core as provided in appendix A of the NIST *Framework for Improving Critical Infrastructure Cybersecurity*.

Function	Category	Subcategory	Informative References
IDENTIFY (ID)	**Asset Management (ID.AM):** The data, personnel, devices, systems, and facilities that enable the organization to achieve business purposes are identified and managed consistent with their relative importance to business objectives and the organization's risk strategy.	**ID.AM-1:** Physical devices and systems within the organization are inventoried.	• **CCS CSC** 1 • **COBIT 5** BAI09.01, BAI09.02 • **ISA 62443-2-1:2009** 4.2.3.4 • **ISA 62443-3-3:2013** SR 7.8 • **ISO/IEC 27001:2013** A.8.1.1, A.8.1.2 • **NIST SP 800-53 Rev. 4** CM-8
		ID.AM-2: Software platforms and applications within the organization are inventoried.	• **CCS CSC** 2 • **COBIT 5** BAI09.01, BAI09.02, BAI09.05 • **ISA 62443-2-1:2009** 4.2.3.4 • **ISA 62443-3-3:2013** SR 7.8 • **ISO/IEC 27001:2013** A.8.1.1, A.8.1.2 • **NIST SP 800-53 Rev. 4** CM-8
		ID.AM-3: Organizational communication and data flows are mapped.	• **CCS CSC** 1 • **COBIT 5** DSS05.02 • **ISA 62443-2-1:2009** 4.2.3.4 • **ISO/IEC 27001:2013** A.13.2.1 • **NIST SP 800-53 Rev. 4** AC-4, CA-3, CA-9, PL-8
		ID.AM-4: External information systems are catalogued.	• **COBIT 5** APO02.02 • **ISO/IEC 27001:2013** A.11.2.6 • **NIST SP 800-53 Rev. 4** AC-20, SA-9
		ID.AM-5: Resources (e.g., hardware, devices, data, and software) are prioritized based on their classification, criticality, and business value.	• **COBIT 5** APO03.03, APO03.04, BAI09.02 • **ISA 62443-2-1:2009** 4.2.3.6 • **ISO/IEC 27001:2013** A.8.2.1 • **NIST SP 800-53 Rev. 4** CP-2, RA-2, SA-14
		ID.AM-6: Cybersecurity roles and responsibilities for the entire workforce and third-party stakeholders (e.g., suppliers, customers, partners) are established.	• **COBIT 5** APO01.02, DSS06.03 • **ISA 62443-2-1:2009** 4.3.2.3.3 • **ISO/IEC 27001:2013** A.6.1.1 • **NIST SP 800-53 Rev. 4** CP-2, PS-7, PM-11

Function	Category	Subcategory	Informative References
IDENTIFY (ID)	**Business Environment (ID.BE):** The organization's mission, objectives, stakeholders, and activities are understood and prioritized; this information is used to inform cybersecurity roles, responsibilities, and risk management decisions.	**ID.BE-1:** The organization's role in the supply chain is identified and communicated.	• **COBIT 5** APO08.04, APO08.05, APO10.03, APO10.04, APO10.05 • **ISO/IEC 27001:2013** A.15.1.3, A.15.2.1, A.15.2.2 • **NIST SP 800-53 Rev. 4** CP-2, SA-12
		ID.BE-2: The organization's place in critical infrastructure and its industry sector is identified and communicated.	• **COBIT 5** APO02.06, APO03.01 • **NIST SP 800-53 Rev. 4** PM-8
		ID.BE-3: Priorities for organizational mission, objectives, and activities are established and communicated.	• **COBIT 5** APO02.01, APO02.06, APO03.01 • **ISA 62443-2-1:2009** 4.2.2.1, 4.2.3.6 • **NIST SP 800-53 Rev. 4** PM-11, SA-14
		ID.BE-4: Dependencies and critical functions for delivery of critical services are established.	• **ISO/IEC 27001:2013** A.11.2.2, A.11.2.3, A.12.1.3 • **NIST SP 800-53 Rev. 4** CP-8, PE-9, PE-11, PM-8, SA-14
		ID.BE-5: Resilience requirements to support delivery of critical services are established.	• **COBIT 5** DSS04.02 • **ISO/IEC 27001:2013** A.11.1.4, A.17.1.1, A.17.1.2, A.17.2.1 • **NIST SP 800-53 Rev. 4** CP-2, CP-11, SA-14
	Governance (ID.GV): The policies, procedures, and processes to manage and monitor the organization's regulatory, legal, risk, environmental, and operational requirements are understood and inform the management of cybersecurity risk.	**ID.GV-1:** Organizational information security policy is established.	• **COBIT 5** APO01.03, EDM01.01, EDM01.02 • **ISA 62443-2-1:2009** 4.3.2.6 • **ISO/IEC 27001:2013** A.5.1.1 • **NIST SP 800-53 Rev. 4** -1 controls from all families
		ID.GV-2: Information security roles and responsibilities are coordinated and aligned with internal roles and external partners.	• **COBIT 5** APO13.12 • **ISA 62443-2-1:2009** 4.3.2.3.3 • **ISO/IEC 27001:2013** A.6.1.1, A.7.2.1 • **NIST SP 800-53 Rev. 4** PM-1, PS-7

Function	Category	Subcategory	Informative References
IDENTIFY (ID)	**Governance (ID.GV):** The policies, procedures, and processes to manage and monitor the organization's regulatory, legal, risk, environmental, and operational requirements are understood and inform the management of cybersecurity risk.	**ID.GV-3:** Legal and regulatory requirements regarding cybersecurity, including privacy and civil liberties obligations, are understood and managed.	• **COBIT 5** MEA03.01, MEA03.04 • **ISA 62443-2-1:2009** 4.4.3.7 • **ISO/IEC 27001:2013** A.18.1 • **NIST SP 800-53 Rev. 4** -1 controls from all families (except PM-1)
		ID.GV-4: Governance and risk management processes address cybersecurity risks.	• **COBIT 5** DSS04.02 • **ISA 62443-2-1:2009** 4.2.3.1, 4.2.3.3, 4.2.3.8, 4.2.3.9, 4.2.3.11, 4.3.2.4.3, 4.3.2.6.3 • **NIST SP 800-53 Rev. 4** PM-9, PM-11
	Risk Assessment (ID.RA): The organization understands the cybersecurity risk to organizational operations (including mission, functions, image, or reputation), organizational assets, and individuals.	**ID.RA-1:** Asset vulnerabilities are identified and documented.	• **CCS CSC** 4 • **COBIT 5** APO12.01, APO12.02, APO12.03, APO12.04 • **ISA 62443-2-1:2009** 4.2.3, 4.2.3.7, 4.2.3.9, 4.2.3.12 • **ISO/IEC 27001:2013** A.12.6.1, A.18.2.3 • **NIST SP 800-53 Rev. 4** CA-2, CA-7, CA-8, RA-3, RA-5, SA-5, SA-11, SI-2, SI-4, SI-5
		ID.RA-2: Threat and vulnerability information is received from information sharing forums and sources.	• **ISA 62443-2-1:2009** 4.2.3, 4.2.3.9, 4.2.3.12 • **ISO/IEC 27001:2013** A.6.1.4 • **NIST SP 800-53 Rev. 4** PM-15, PM-16, SI-5
		ID.RA-3: Threats, both internal and external, are identified and documented.	• **COBIT 5** APO12.01, APO12.02, APO12.03, APO12.04 • **ISA 62443-2-1:2009** 4.2.3, 4.2.3.9, 4.2.3.12 • **NIST SP 800-53 Rev. 4** RA-3, SI-5, PM-12, PM-16
		ID.RA-4: Potential business impacts and likelihoods are identified.	• **COBIT 5** DSS04.02 • **ISA 62443-2-1:2009** 4.2.3, 4.2.3.9, 4.2.3.12 • **NIST SP 800-53 Rev. 4** RA-2, RA-3, PM-9, PM-11, SA-14

Function	Category	Subcategory	Informative References
IDENTIFY (ID)	**Risk Assessment (ID.RA):** The organization understands the cybersecurity risk to organizational operations (including mission, functions, image, or reputation), organizational assets, and individuals.	**ID.RA-5:** Threats, vulnerabilities, likelihoods, and impacts are used to determine risk.	• **COBIT 5** APO12.02 • **ISO/IEC 27001:2013** A.12.6.1 • **NIST SP 800-53 Rev. 4** RA-2, RA-3, PM-16
		ID.RA-6: Risk responses are identified and prioritized.	• **COBIT 5** APO12.05, APO13.02 • **NIST SP 800-53 Rev. 4** PM-4, PM-9
	Risk Management Strategy (ID.RM): The organization's priorities, constraints, risk tolerances, and assumptions are established and used to support operational risk decisions.	**ID.RM-1:** Risk management processes are established, managed, and agreed to by organizational stakeholders.	• **COBIT 5** APO12.04, APO12.05, APO13.02, BAI02.03, BAI04.02 • **ISA 62443-2-1:2009** 4.3.4.2 • **NIST SP 800-53 Rev. 4** PM-9
		ID.RM-2: Organizational risk tolerance is determined and clearly expressed.	• **COBIT 5** APO12.06 • **ISA 62443-2-1:2009** 4.3.2.6.5 • **NIST SP 800-53 Rev. 4** PM-9
		ID.RM-3: The organization's determination of risk tolerance is informed by its role in critical infrastructure and sector specific risk analysis.	• **NIST SP 800-53 Rev. 4** PM-8, PM-9, PM-11, SA-14
PROTECT (PR)	**Access Control (PR.AC):** Access to assets and associated facilities is limited to authorized users, processes, or devices, and to authorized activities and transactions.	**PR.AC-1:** Identities and credentials are managed for authorized devices and users.	• **CCS CSC** 16 • **COBIT 5** DSS05.04, DSS06.03 • **ISA 62443-2-1:2009** 4.3.3.5.1 • **ISA 62443-3-3:2013** SR 1.1, SR 1.2, SR 1.3, SR 1.4, SR 1.5, SR 1.7, SR 1.8, SR 1.9 • **ISO/IEC 27001:2013** A.9.2.1, A.9.2.2, A.9.2.4, A.9.3.1, A.9.4.2, A.9.4.3 • **NIST SP 800-53 Rev. 4** AC-2, IA Family
		PR.AC-2: Physical access to assets is managed and protected.	• **COBIT 5** DSS01.04, DSS05.05 • **ISA 62443-2-1:2009** 4.3.3.3.2, 4.3.3.3.8 • **ISO/IEC 27001:2013** A.11.1.1, A.11.1.2, A.11.1.4, A.11.1.6, A.11.2.3 • **NIST SP 800-53 Rev. 4** PE-2, PE-3, PE-4, PE-5, PE-6, PE-9

Function	Category	Subcategory	Informative References
PROTECT (PR)	**Access Control (PR.AC)**: Access to assets and associated facilities is limited to authorized users, processes, or devices, and to authorized activities and transactions.	**PR.AC-3**: Remote access is managed	• **COBIT 5** APO13.01, DSS01.04, DSS05.03 • **ISA 62443-2-1:2009** 4.3.3.6.6 • **ISA 62443-3-3:2013** SR 1.13, SR 2.6 • **ISO/IEC 27001:2013** A.6.2.2, A.13.1.1, A.13.2.1 • **NIST SP 800-53 Rev. 4** AC 17, AC-19, AC-20
		PR.AC-4: Access permissions are managed, incorporating the principles of least privilege and separation of duties.	• **CCS CSC** 12, 15 • **ISA 62443-2-1:2009** 4.3.3.7.3 • **ISA 62443-3-3:2013** SR 2.1 • **ISO/IEC 27001:2013** A.6.1.2, A.9.1.2, A.9.2.3, A.9.4.1, A.9.4.4 • **NIST SP 800-53 Rev. 4** AC-2, AC-3, AC-5, AC-6, AC-16
		PR.AC-5: Network integrity is protected, incorporating network segregation where appropriate.	• **ISA 62443-2-1:2009** 4.3.3.4 • **ISA 62443-3-3:2013** SR 3.1, SR 3.8 • **ISO/IEC 27001:2013** A.13.1.1, A.13.1.3, A.13.2.1 • **NIST SP 800-53 Rev. 4** AC-4, SC-7
	Awareness and Training (PR.AT): The organization's personnel and partners are provided cybersecurity awareness education and are adequately trained to perform their information security-related duties and responsibilities consistent with related policies, procedures, and agreements.	**PR.AT-1**: All users are informed and trained.	• **CCS CSC** 9 • **COBIT 5** APO07.03, BAI05.07 • **ISA 62443-2-1:2009** 4.3.2.4.2 • **ISO/IEC 27001:2013** A.7.2.2 • **NIST SP 800-53 Rev. 4** AT-2, PM-13

Function	Category	Subcategory	Informative References
PROTECT (PR)	**Awareness and Training (PR.AT):** The organization's personnel and partners are provided cybersecurity awareness education and are adequately trained to perform their information security-related duties and responsibilities consistent with related policies, procedures, and agreements.	**PR.AT-2:** Privileged users understand roles and responsibilities.	• **CCS CSC** 9 • **COBIT 5** APO07.02, DSS06.03 • **ISA 62443-2-1:2009** 4.3.2.4.2, 4.3.2.4.3 • **ISO/IEC 27001:2013** A.6.1.1, A.7.2.2 • **NIST SP 800-53 Rev. 4** AT-3, PM-13
		PR.AT-3: Third-party stakeholders (e.g., suppliers, customers, partners) understand roles and responsibilities.	• **CCS CSC** 9 • **COBIT 5** APO07.03, APO10.04, APO10.05 • **ISA 62443-2-1:2009** 4.3.2.4.2 • **ISO/IEC 27001:2013** A.6.1.1, A.7.2.2 • **NIST SP 800-53 Rev. 4** PS-7, SA-9
		PR.AT-4: Senior executives understand roles and responsibilities.	• **CCS CSC** 9 • **COBIT 5** APO07.03 • **ISA 62443-2-1:2009** 4.3.2.4.2 • **ISO/IEC 27001:2013** A.6.1.1, A.7.2.2, • **NIST SP 800-53 Rev. 4** AT-3, PM-13
		PR.AT-5: Physical and information security personnel understand roles and responsibilities.	• **CCS CSC** 9 • **COBIT 5** APO07.03 • **ISA 62443-2-1:2009** 4.3.2.4.2 • **ISO/IEC 27001:2013** A.6.1.1, A.7.2.2, • **NIST SP 800-53 Rev. 4** AT-3, PM-13
	Data Security (PR.DS): Information and records (data) are managed consistent with the organization's risk strategy to protect the confidentiality, integrity, and availability of information.	**PR.DS-1:** Data-at-rest is protected.	• **CCS CSC** 17 • **COBIT 5** APO01.06, BAI02.01, BAI06.01, DSS06.06 • **ISA 62443-3-3:2013** SR 3.4, SR 4.1 • **ISO/IEC 27001:2013** A.8.2.3 • **NIST SP 800-53 Rev. 4** SC-28

Function	Category	Subcategory	Informative References
PROTECT (PR)	Data Security (PR.DS): Information and records (data) are managed consistent with the organization's risk strategy to protect the confidentiality, integrity, and availability of information.	PR.DS-2: Data-in-transit is protected.	• CCS CSC 17 • COBIT 5 APO01.06, DSS06.06 • ISA 62443-3-3:2013 SR 3.1, SR 3.8, SR 4.1, SR 4.2 • ISO/IEC 27001:2013 A.8.2.3, A.13.1.1, A.13.2.1, A.13.2.3, A.14.1.2, A.14.1.3 • NIST SP 800-53 Rev. 4 SC-8
		PR.DS-3: Assets are formally managed throughout removal, transfers, and disposition.	• COBIT 5 BAI09.03 • ISA 62443-2-1:2009 4.4.3.3.9, 4.3.4.4.1 • ISA 62443-3-3:2013 SR 4.2 • ISO/IEC 27001:2013 A.8.2.3, A.8.3.1, A.8.3.2, A.8.3.3, A.11.2.7 • NIST SP 800-53 Rev. 4 CM-8, MP-6, PE-16
		PR.DS-4: Adequate capacity to ensure availability is maintained.	• COBIT 5 APO13.01 • ISA 62443-3-3:2013 SR 7.1, SR 7.2 • ISO/IEC 27001:2013 A.12.3.1 • NIST SP 800-53 Rev. 4 AU-4, CP-2, SC-5
		PR.DS-5: Protections against data leaks are implemented.	• CCS CSC 17 • COBIT 5 APO01.06 • ISA 62443-3-3:2013 SR 5.2 • ISO/IEC 27001:2013 A.6.1.2, A.7.1.1, A.7.1.2, A.7.3.1, A.8.2.2, A.8.2.3, A.9.1.1, A.9.1.2, A.9.2.3, A.9.4.1, A.9.4.4, A.9.4.5, A.13.1.3, A.13.2.1, A.13.2.3, A.13.2.4, A.14.1.2, A.14.1.3 • NIST SP 800-53 Rev. 4 AC-4, AC-5, AC-6, PE-19, PS-3, PS-6, SC-7, SC-8, SC-13, SC-31, SI-4

Function	Category	Subcategory	Informative References
PROTECT (PR)	**Data Security (PR.DS):** Information and records (data) are managed consistent with the organization's risk strategy to protect the confidentiality, integrity, and availability of information.	**PR.DS-6:** Integrity checking mechanisms are used to verify software, firmware, and information integrity.	• **ISA 62443-3-3:2013** SR 3.1, SR 3.3, SR 3.4, SR 3.8 • **ISO/IEC 27001:2013** A.12.2.1, A.12.5.1, A.14.1.2, A.14.1.3 • **NIST SP 800-53 Rev. 4** SI-7
		PR.DS-7: The development and testing environment(s) are separate from the production environment.	• **COBIT 5** BAI07.04 • **ISO/IEC 27001:2013** A.12.1.4 • **NIST SP 800-53 Rev. 4** CM-2
	Information Protection Processes and Procedures (PR.IP): Security policies (that address purpose, scope, roles, responsibilities, management commitment, and coordination among organizational entities), processes, and procedures are maintained and used to manage protection of information systems and assets.	**PR.IP-1:** A baseline configuration of information technology/industrial control systems is created and maintained.	• **CCS CSC** 3, 10 • **COBIT 5** BAI10.01, BAI10.02, BAI10.03, BAI10.05 • **ISA 62443-2-1:2009** 4.3.4.3.2, 4.3.4.3.3 • **ISA 62443-3-3:2013** SR 7.6 • **ISO/IEC 27001:2013** A.12.1.2, A.12.5.1, A.12.6.2, A.14.2.2, A.14.2.3, A.14.2.4 • **NIST SP 800-53 Rev. 4** CM-2, CM-3, CM-4, CM-5, CM-6, CM-7, CM-9, SA-10
		PR.IP-2: A System Development Life Cycle to manage systems is implemented.	• **COBIT 5** AP013.01 • **ISA 62443-2-1:2009** 4.3.4.3.3 • **ISO/IEC 27001:2013** A.6.1.5, A.14.1.1, A.14.2.1, A.14.2.5 • **NIST SP 800-53 Rev. 4** SA-3, SA-4, SA-8, SA-10, SA-11, SA-12, SA-15, SA-17, PL-8
		PR.IP-3: Configuration change control processes are in place.	• **COBIT 5** BAI06.01, BAI01.06 • **ISA 62443-2-1:2009** 4.3.4.3.2, 4.3.4.3.3 • **ISA 62443-3-3:2013** SR 7.6 • **ISO/IEC 27001:2013** A.12.1.2, A.12.5.1, A.12.6.2, A.14.2.2, A.14.2.3, A.14.2.4 • **NIST SP 800-53 Rev. 4** CM-3, CM-4, SA-10

Function	Category	Subcategory	Informative References
PROTECT (PR)	**Information Protection Processes and Procedures (PR.IP):** Security policies (that address purpose, scope, roles, responsibilities, management commitment, and coordination among organizational entities), processes, and procedures are maintained and used to manage protection of information systems and assets.	**PR.IP-4:** Backups of information are conducted, maintained, and tested periodically.	• **COBIT 5** APO13.01 • **ISA 62443-2-1:2009** 4.3.4.3.9 • **ISA 62443-3-3:2013** SR 7.3, SR 7.4 • **ISO/IEC 27001:2013** A.12.3.1, A.17.1.2A.17.1.3, A.18.1.3 • **NIST SP 800-53 Rev. 4** CP-4, CP-6, CP-9
		PR.IP-5: Policy and regulations regarding the physical operating environment for organizational assets are met.	• **COBIT 5** DSS01.04, DSS05.05 • **ISA 62443-2-1:2009** 4.3.3.3.1 4.3.3.3.2, 4.3.3.3, 4.3.3.3.5, 4.3.3.3.6 • **ISO/IEC 27001:2013** A.11.1.4, A.11.2.1, A.11.2.2, A.11.2.3 • **NIST SP 800-53 Rev. 4** PE-10, PE-12, PE-13, PE-14, PE-15, PE-18
		PR.IP-6: Data is destroyed according to policy.	• **COBIT 5** BAI09.03 • **ISA 62443-2-1:2009** 4.3.4.4.4 • **ISA 62443-3-3:2013** SR 4.2 • **ISO/IEC 27001:2013** A.8.2.3, A.8.3.1, A.8.3.2, A.11.2.7 • **NIST SP 800-53 Rev. 4** MP-6
		PR.IP-7: Protection processes are continuously improved.	• **COBIT 5** APO11.06, DSS04.05 • **ISA 62443-2-1:2009** 4.4.3.1, 4.4.3.2, 4.4.3.3, 4.4.3.4, 4.4.3.5, 4.4.3.6, 4.4.3.7, 4.4.3.8 • **NIST SP 800-53 Rev. 4** CA-2, CA-7, CP-2, IR-8, PL-2, PM-6
		PR.IP-8: Effectiveness of protection technologies is shared with appropriate parties.	• **ISO/IEC 27001:2013** A.16.1.6 • **NIST SP 800-53 Rev. 4** AC-21, CA-7, SI-4

Function	Category	Subcategory	Informative References
PROTECT (PR)	**Information Protection Processes and Procedures (PR.IP):** Security policies (that address purpose, scope, roles, responsibilities, management commitment, and coordination among organizational entities), processes, and procedures are maintained and used to manage protection of information systems and assets.	**PR.IP-9:** Response plans (Incident Response and Business Continuity) and recovery plans (Incident Recovery and Disaster Recovery) are in place and managed.	• **COBIT 5** DSS04.03 • **ISA 62443-2-1:2009** 4.3.2.5.3, 4.3.4.5.1 • **ISO/IEC 27001:2013** A.16.1.1, A.17.1.1, A.17.1.2 • **NIST SP 800-53 Rev. 4** CP-2, IR-8
		PR.IP-10: Response and recovery plans are tested.	• **ISA 62443-2-1:2009** 4.3.2.5.7, 4.3.4.5.11 • **ISA 62443-3-3:2013** SR 3.3 • **ISO/IEC 27001:2013** A.17.1.3 • **NIST SP 800-53 Rev.4** CP-4, IR-3, PM-14
		PR.IP-11: Cybersecurity is included in human resources practices (e.g., deprovisioning, personnel screening).	• **COBIT 5** AP007.01, AP007.02, AP007.03, AP007.04, AP007.05 • **ISA 62443-2-1:2009** 4.3.3.2.1, 4.3.3.2.2, 4.3.3.2.3 • **ISO/IEC 27001:2013** A.7.1.1, A.7.3.1, A.8.1.4 • **NIST SP 800-53 Rev. 4** PS Family
		PR.IP-12: A vulnerability management plan is developed and implemented.	• **ISO/IEC 27001:2013** A.12.6.1, A.18.2.2 • **NIST SP 800-53 Rev. 4** RA-3, RA-5, SI-2
	Maintenance (PR.MA): Maintenance and repairs of industrial control and information system components is performed consistent with policies and procedures.	**PR.MA-1:** Maintenance and repair of organizational assets is performed and logged in a timely manner, with approved and controlled tools.	• **COBIT 5** BAI09.03 • **ISA 62443-2-1:2009** 4.3.3.3.7 • **ISO/IEC 27001:2013** A.11.1.2, A.11.2.4, A.11.2.5 • **NIST SP 800-53 Rev. 4** MA-2, MA-3, MA-5
		PR.MA-2: Remote maintenance of organizational assets is approved, logged, and performed in a manner that prevents unauthorized access.	• **COBIT 5** DSS05.04 • **ISA 62443-2-1:2009** 4.3.3.6.5, 4.3.3.6.6, 4.3.3.6.7, 4.4.4.6.8 • **ISO/IEC 27001:2013** A.11.2.4, A.15.1.1, A.15.2.1 • **NIST SP 800-53 Rev. 4** MA-4

Function	Category	Subcategory	Informative References
PROTECT (PR)	**Protective Technology (PR.PT):** Technical security solutions are managed to ensure the security and resilience of systems and assets, consistent with related policies, procedures, and agreements.	**PR.PT-1:** Audit/log records are determined, documented, implemented, and reviewed in accordance with policy.	• **CCS CSC** 14 • **COBIT 5** APO11.04 • **ISA 62443-2-1:2009** 4.3.3.3.9, 4.3.3.5.8, 4.3.4.4.7, 4.4.2.1, 4.4.2.2, 4.4.2.4 • **ISA 62443-3-3:2013** SR 2.8, SR 2.9, SR 2.10, SR 2.11, SR 2.12 • **ISO/IEC 27001:2013** A.12.4.1, A.12.4.2, A.12.4.3, A.12.4.4, A.12.7.1 • **NIST SP 800-53 Rev. 4** AU Family
		PR.PT-2: Removable media is protected and its use restricted according to policy.	• **COBIT 5** DSS05.02, APO13.01 • **ISA 62443-3-3:2013** SR 2.3 • **ISO/IEC 27001:2013** A.8.2.2, A.8.2.3, A.8.3.1, A.8.3.3, A.11.2.9 • **NIST SP 800-53 Rev. 4** MP-2, MP-4, MP-5, MP-7
		PR.PT-3: Access to systems and assets is controlled, incorporating the principle of least functionality.	• **COBIT 5** DSS05.02 • **ISA 62443-2-1:2009** 4.3.3.5.1, 4.3.3.5.2, 4.3.3.5.3, 4.3.3.5.4, 4.3.3.5.5, 4.3.3.5.6, 4.3.3.5.7, 4.3.3.5.8, 4.3.3.6.1, 4.3.3.6.2, 4.3.3.6.3, 4.3.3.6.4, 4.3.3.6.5, 4.3.3.6.6, 4.3.3.6.7, 4.3.3.6.8, 4.3.3.6.9, 4.3.3.7.1, 4.3.3.7.2, 4.3.3.7.3, 4.3.3.7.4 • **ISA 62443-3-3:2013** SR 1.1, SR 1.2, SR 1.3, SR 1.4, SR 1.5, SR 1.6, SR 1.7, SR 1.8, SR 1.9, SR 1.10, SR 1.11, SR 1.12, SR 1.13, SR 2.1, SR 2.2, SR 2.3, SR 2.4, SR 2.5, SR 2.6, SR 2.7 • **ISO/IEC 27001:2013** A.9.1.2 • **NIST SP 800-53 Rev. 4** AC-3, CM-7

Function	Category	Subcategory	Informative References
PROTECT (PR)	**Protective Technology (PR.PT):** Technical security solutions are managed to ensure the security and resilience of systems and assets, consistent with related policies, procedures, and agreements.	**PR.PT-4:** Communications and control networks are protected.	• **CCS CSC** 7 • **COBIT 5** DSS05.02, APO13.01 • **ISA 62443-3-3:2013** SR 3.1, SR 3.5, SR 3.8, SR 4.1, SR 4.3, SR 5.1, SR 5.2, SR 5.3, SR 7.1, SR 7.6 • **ISO/IEC 27001:2013** A.13.1.1, A.13.2.1 • **NIST SP 800-53 Rev. 4** AC-4, AC-17, AC-18, CP-8, SC-7
DETECT (DE)	**Anomalies and Events (DE.AE):** Anomalous activity is detected in a timely manner and the potential impact of events is understood.	**DE.AE-1:** A baseline of network operations and expected data flows for users and systems is established and managed.	• **COBIT 5** DSS03.01 • **ISA 62443-2-1:2009** 4.4.3.3 • **NIST SP 800-53 Rev. 4** AC-4, CA-3, CM-2, SI-4
		DE.AE-2: Detected events are analyzed to understand attack targets and methods.	• **ISA 62443-2-1:2009** 4.3.4.5.6, 4.3.4.5.7, 4.3.4.5.8 • **ISA 62443-3-3:2013** SR 2.8, SR 2.9, SR 2.10, SR 2.11, SR 2.12, SR 3.9, SR 6.2 • **ISO/IEC 27001:2013** A.16.1.1, A.16.1.4 • **NIST SP 800-53 Rev. 4** AU-6, CA-7, IR-4, SI-4
		DE.AE-3: Event data are aggregated and correlated from multiple sources and sensors.	• **ISA 62443-3-3:2013** SR 6.1 • **NIST SP 800-53 Rev. 4** AU-6, CA-7, IR-4, IR-5, IR-8, SI-4
		DE.AE-4: Impact of events is determined.	• **COBIT 5** APO12.06 • **NIST SP 800-53 Rev. 4** CP-2, IR-4, RA-3, SI-4
		DE.AE-5: Incident alert thresholds are established.	• **COBIT 5** APO12.06 • **ISA 62443-2-1:2009** 4.2.3.10 • **NIST SP 800-53 Rev. 4** IR-4, IR-5, IR-8
	Security Continuous Monitoring (DE. CM): The information system and assets are monitored at discrete intervals to identify cybersecurity events and verify the effectiveness of protective measures.	**DE.CM-1:** The network is monitored to detect potential cybersecurity events.	• **CCS CSC** 14, 16 • **COBIT 5** DSS05.07 • **ISA 62443-3-3:2013** SR 6.2 • **NIST SP 800-53 Rev. 4** AC-2, AU-12, CA-7, CM-3, SC-5, SC-7, SI-4

Function	Category	Subcategory	Informative References
DETECT (DE)	**Security Continuous Monitoring (DE.CM):** The information system and assets are monitored at discrete intervals to identify cybersecurity events and verify the effectiveness of protective measures.	**DE.CM-2:** The physical environment is monitored to detect potential cybersecurity events.	• **ISA 62443-2-1:2009** 4.3.3.3.8 • **NIST SP 800-53 Rev. 4** CA-7, PE-3, PE-6, PE-20
		DE.CM-3: Personnel activity is monitored to detect potential cybersecurity events.	• **ISA 62443-3-3:2013** SR 6.2 • **ISO/IEC 27001:2013** A.12.4.1 • **NIST SP 800-53 Rev. 4** AC-2, AU-12, AU-13, CA-7, CM-10, CM-11
		DE.CM-4: Malicious code is detected.	• **CCS CSC** 5 • **COBIT 5** DSS05.01 • **ISA 62443-2-1:2009** 4.3.4.3.8 • **ISA 62443-3-3:2013** SR 3.2 • **ISO/IEC 27001:2013** A.12.2.1 • **NIST SP 800-53 Rev. 4** SI-3
		DE.CM-5: Unauthorized mobile code is detected.	• **ISA 62443-3-3:2013** SR 2.4 • **ISO/IEC 27001:2013** A.12.5.1 • **NIST SP 800-53 Rev. 4** SC-18, SI-4, SC-44
		DE.CM-6: External service provider activity is monitored to detect potential cybersecurity events.	• **COBIT 5** APO07.06 • **ISO/IEC 27001:2013** A.14.2.7, A.15.2.1 • **NIST SP 800-53 Rev. 4** CA-7, PS-7, SA-4, SA-9, SI-4
		DE.CM-7: Monitoring for unauthorized personnel, connections, devices, and software is performed.	• **NIST SP 800-53 Rev. 4** AU-12, CA-7, CM-3, CM-8, PE-3, PE-6, PE-20, SI-4
		DE.CM-8: Vulnerability scans are performed.	• **COBIT 5** BAI03.10 • **ISA 62443-2-1:2009** 4.2.3.1, 4.2.3.7 • **ISO/IEC 27001:2013** A.12.6.1 • **NIST SP 800-53 Rev. 4** RA-5

Function	Category	Subcategory	Informative References
DETECT (DE)	**Detection Processes (DE.DP):** Detection processes and procedures are maintained and tested to ensure timely and adequate awareness of anomalous events.	**DE.DP-1:** Roles and responsibilities for detection are well defined to ensure accountability.	• **CCS CSC** 5 • **COBIT 5** DSS05.01 • **ISA 62443-2-1:2009** 4.4.3.1 • **ISO/IEC 27001:2013** A.6.1.1 • **NIST SP 800-53 Rev. 4** CA-2, CA-7, PM-14
		DE.DP-2: Detection activities comply with all applicable requirements.	• **ISA 62443-2-1:2009** 4.4.3.2 • **ISO/IEC 27001:2013** A.18.1.4 • **NIST SP 800-53 Rev. 4** CA-2, CA-7, PM-14, SI-4
		DE.DP-3: Detection processes are tested.	• **COBIT 5** APO13.02 • **ISA 62443-2-1:2009** 4.4.3.2 • **ISA 62443-3-3:2013** SR 3.3 • **ISO/IEC 27001:2013** A.14.2.8 • **NIST SP 800-53 Rev. 4** CA-2, CA-7, PE-3, PM-14, SI-3, SI-4
		DE.DP-4: Event detection information is communicated to appropriate parties.	• **COBIT 5** APO12.06 • **ISA 62443-2-1:2009** 4.3.4.5.9 • **ISA 62443-3-3:2013** SR 6.1 • **ISO/IEC 27001:2013** A.16.1.2 • **NIST SP 800-53 Rev. 4** AU-6, CA-2, CA-7, RA-5, SI-4
		DE.DP-5: Detection processes are continuously improved	• **COBIT 5** APO11.06, DSS04.05 • **ISA 62443-2-1:2009** 4.4.3.4 • **ISO/IEC 27001:2013** A.16.1.6 • **NIST SP 800-53 Rev. 4**, CA-2, CA-7, PL-2, RA-5, SI-4, PM-14

Function	Category	Subcategory	Informative References
RESPOND (RS)	**Response Planning (RS.RP):** Response processes and procedures are executed and maintained, to ensure timely response to detected cybersecurity events.	**RS.RP-1:** Response plan is executed during or after an event.	• **COBIT 5** BAI01.10 • **CCS CSC** 18 • **ISA 62443-2-1:2009** 4.3.4.5.1 • **ISO/IEC 27001:2013** A.16.1.5 • **NIST SP 800-53 Rev. 4** CP-2, CP-10, IR-4, IR-8
	Communications (RS.CO): Response activities are coordinated with internal and external stakeholders, as appropriate, to include external support from law enforcement agencies.	**RS.CO-1:** Personnel know their roles and order of operations when a response is needed.	• **ISA 62443-2-1:2009** 4.3.4.5.2, 4.3.4.5.3, 4.3.4.5.4 • **ISO/IEC 27001:2013** A.6.1.1, A.16.1.1 • **NIST SP 800-53 Rev. 4** CP-2, CP-3, IR-3, IR-8
		RS.CO-2: Events are reported consistent with established criteria.	• **ISA 62443-2-1:2009** 4.3.4.5.5 • **ISO/IEC 27001:2013** A.6.1.3, A.16.1.2 • **NIST SP 800-53 Rev. 4** AU-6, IR-6, IR-8
		RS.CO-3: Information is shared consistent with response plans.	• **ISA 62443-2-1:2009** 4.3.4.5.2 • **ISO/IEC 27001:2013** A.16.1.2 • **NIST SP 800-53 Rev. 4** CA-2, CA-7, CP-2, IR-4, IR-8, PE-6, RA-5, SI-4
		RS.CO-4: Coordination with stakeholders occurs consistent with response plans.	• **ISA 62443-2-1:2009** 4.3.4.5.5 • **NIST SP 800-53 Rev. 4** CP-2, IR-4, IR-8
		RS.CO-5: Voluntary information sharing occurs with external stakeholders to achieve broader cybersecurity situational awareness.	• **NIST SP 800-53 Rev. 4** PM-15, SI-5

Function	Category	Subcategory	Informative References
RESPOND (RS)	Analysis (RS.AN): Analysis is conducted to ensure adequate response and support recovery activities.	RS.AN-1: Notifications from detection systems are investigated.	• COBIT 5 DSS02.07 • ISA 62443-2-1:2009 4.3.4.5.6, 4.3.4.5.7, 4.3.4.5.8 • ISA 62443-3-3:2013 SR 6.1 • ISO/IEC 27001:2013 A.12.4.1, A.12.4.3, A.16.1.5 • NIST SP 800-53 Rev. 4 AU-6, CA-7, IR-4, IR-5, PE-6, SI-4
		RS.AN-2: The impact of the incident is understood.	• ISA 62443-2-1:2009 4.3.4.5.6, 4.3.4.5.7, 4.3.4.5.8 • ISO/IEC 27001:2013 A.16.1.6 • NIST SP 800-53 Rev. 4 CP-2, IR-4
		RS.AN-3: Forensics are performed.	• ISA 62443-3-3:2013 SR 2.8, SR 2.9, SR 2.10, SR 2.11, SR 2.12, SR 3.9, SR 6.1 • ISO/IEC 27001:2013 A.16.1.7 • NIST SP 800-53 Rev. 4 AU-7, IR-4
		RS.AN-4: Incidents are categorized consistent with response plans.	• ISA 62443-2-1:2009 4.3.4.5.6 • ISO/IEC 27001:2013 A.16.1.4 • NIST SP 800-53 Rev. 4 CP-2, IR-4, IR-5, IR-8
	Mitigation (RS.MI): Activities are performed to prevent expansion of an event, mitigate its effects, and eradicate the incident.	RS.MI-1: Incidents are contained.	• ISA 62443-2-1:2009 4.3.4.5.6 • ISA 62443-3-3:2013 SR 5.1, SR 5.2, SR 5.4 • ISO/IEC 27001:2013 A.16.1.5 • NIST SP 800-53 Rev. 4 IR-4
		RS.MI-2: Incidents are mitigated.	• ISA 62443-2-1:2009 4.3.4.5.6, 4.3.4.5.10 • ISO/IEC 27001:2013 A.12.2.1, A.16.1.5 • NIST SP 800-53 Rev. 4 IR-4
		RS.MI-3: Newly identified vulnerabilities are mitigated or documented as accepted risks.	• ISO/IEC 27001:2013 A.12.6.1 • NIST SP 800-53 Rev. 4 CA-7, RA-3, RA-5

Function	Category	Subcategory	Informative References
RESPOND (RS)	**Improvements (RS.IM):** Organizational response activities are improved by incorporating lessons learned from current and previous detection/response activities.	**RS.IM-1:** Response plans incorporate lessons learned.	• **COBIT 5** BAI01.13 • **ISA 62443-2-1:2009** 4.3.4.5.10, 4.4.3.4 • **ISO/IEC 27001:2013** A.16.1.6 • **NIST SP 800-53 Rev. 4** CP-2, IR-4, IR-8
		RS.IM-2: Response strategies are updated.	• **NIST SP 800-53 Rev. 4** CP-2, IR-4, IR-8
RECOVER (RC)	**Recovery Planning (RC.RP):** Recovery processes and procedures are executed and maintained to ensure timely restoration of systems or assets affected by cybersecurity events.	**RC.RP-1:** Recovery plan is executed during or after an event.	• **CCS CSC** 8 • **COBIT 5** DSS02.05, DSS03.04 • **ISO/IEC 27001:2013** A.16.1.5 • **NIST SP 800-53 Rev. 4** CP-10, IR-4, IR-8
	Improvements (RC.IM): Recovery planning and processes are improved by incorporating lessons learned into future activities.	**RC.IM-1:** Recovery plans incorporate lessons learned.	• **COBIT 5** BAI05.07 • **ISA 62443-2-1:2009** 4.4.3.4 • **NIST SP 800-53 Rev. 4** CP-2, IR-4, IR-8
		RC.IM-2: Recovery strategies are updated.	• **COBIT 5** BAI07.08 • **NIST SP 800-53 Rev. 4** CP-2, IR-4, IR-8
	Communications (RC.CO): Restoration activities are coordinated with internal and external parties, such as coordinating centers, Internet Service Providers, owners of attacking systems, victims, other CSIRTs, and vendors.	**RC.CO-1:** Public relations are managed.	• **COBIT 5** EDM03.02
		RC.CO-2: Reputation after an event is repaired.	• **COBIT 5** MEA03.02
		RC.CO-3: Recovery activities are communicated to internal stakeholders and executive and management teams.	• **NIST SP 800-53 Rev. 4** CP-2, IR-4

Source: NIST, *Framework for Improving Critical Infrastructure Cybersecurity*, USA, 2014, Appendix A

Appendix B: Detailed Profile Template

As discussed in chapter 2, the profile template provides a mechanism for tracking the current state of the organization's cybersecurity program and identifies the characteristics of the target state. The subsections of this appendix provide an example template for storing the information regarding the profile, the current state profile template and target state profile template.

Profile Metadata

The profile metadata table, shown in **figure B.1**, is used to capture information regarding the organization and the business unit or system(s) that are represented by the profile. This information is typically collected in phases 1 and 2 of the CSF implementation process.

Figure B.1—Profile Metadata Template	
Organization	
Critical Infrastructure Sector	
Organization Business Unit/Sector/Subsidiary (if applicable)	
Organization Current Profile Scope	
Business Requirements	1. 2. 3. 4.
Risk Considerations	
Risk Appetite Decisions	

Current State Profile

The current state profile is used to track the goals of the current cybersecurity program. The template includes a capability to identify how each subcategory within the framework is being obtained and the current implementation status of that capability. In many cases, organizations update their current security policy and implement the new policy in a phased approach. The current state profile template allows organizations to accurately represent their status in implementing current policies and procedures. **Figure B.2** identifies the data points or topics recorded in the current state profile. The full Current Profile template is available in Microsoft Excel® format in a tool kit from ISACA.

Figure B.2—Current Profile Data Points	
Topic	**Required Information**
Function	Applicable Framework Function
Category	Applicable Framework Category
Subcategory	Applicable Framework Subcategory
Relevant COBIT Processes	The COBIT 5 informative reference used to identify the organizational practices required to meet the goals of the CSF subcategory
Implementation Status	The current achievement rating (i.e., Not achieved, Partially achieved, Largely achieved, Fully achieved) based on the current implementation of existing policies and procedures
Organizational Practices	The organizational practice, policy or procedure that is required to meet the intended goal of the subcategory
Comments/Evidence	Narrative describing how the achievement rating was determined and any established ongoing actions toward the goal of the subcategory

Target State Profile

The target state profile provides an opportunity to capture the desired state of the cybersecurity program. The target state profile should be completed in a manner that identifies the protections and capabilities required to mitigate threats to the organization. This risk-based approach ensures that all areas of the CSF are addressed, with a focus being applied to those areas most likely to be attacked. The full Target Profile template is available in Microsoft Excel format in a tool kit from ISACA. Target profile data points are shown in **figure B.3**.

Figure B.3—Target Profile Data Points	
Topic	**Required Information**
Function	Applicable Framework Function
Category	Applicable Framework Category
Subcategory	Applicable Framework Subcategory
Relevant COBIT Processes	The COBIT 5 informative reference used to identify the organizational practices required to meet the goals of the CSF subcategory
Implementation Status	The achievement rating (i.e. Not Achieved, Partially achieved, Largely achieved, Fully achieved) based on the implementation of existing policies and procedures
Organizational Practices	The organizational practice, policy or procedure identified through the risk-based assessment of organizational needs to mitigate organizational risk related to the category
Comments/Evidence	Narrative describing how the achievement rating was determined and any established ongoing actions toward the goal of the subcategory
Recommended Actions	The actions required to achieve the target state goals
Resource Required	Organizational resources required to complete the recommended actions

Gap Analysis

For each of the subcategories in the Target Profile, consider the difference between the target level of achievement and the current level. Understanding the gaps between the current and target organizational policies and practices will highlight opportunities for improvement; understanding the relative impact on risk will help establish priority, schedule, and resource allocation. Using the information from the gap analysis, conduct the Activity Planning. Detailed Activity Planning guidance is provided in Appendix D and an example Action Planning template is available in Microsoft Excel format in a tool kit from ISACA.

Page intentionally left blank

Appendix C: Framework Cover Letter

In August 2013, NIST provided an open letter to senior executives on the CSF.[8] This open letter introduced the concepts of the initial vision for the CSF. Many of these points were achieved in the final framework. The letter is provided below as a reference and to provide perspectives on the intent of the CSF.

Discussion Draft: Message to Senior Executives on the Cybersecurity Framework

The national and economic security of the United States depends on the reliable functioning of critical infrastructure. The complexity of our systems, the increased connectivity, and the reliance on technology coupled with an advancing cybersecurity threat now puts our critical infrastructure, our information, and our safety at risk. The cybersecurity threat to critical infrastructure continues to grow and represents one of the most serious national security challenges we must confront. This risk not only affects the nation, but also your business, your employees and the communities that you serve.

Cybersecurity risk is a reality that organizations must understand and manage to the level of fidelity of other business risks that can have critical impacts. Much like reputational, financial, supplier, and other risks, organizations must manage cybersecurity risk in order to gain and maintain customers, reduce cost, increase revenue, and innovate. If your company is publicly traded, for example, your Board of Directors should be aware of cybersecurity risk and the steps your organization must take to manage this risk.

The potential consequences of a cybersecurity incident vary — the impact ranges from the loss of valuable intellectual property to the disruption of critical service delivery. Active threats seek to steal information, destroy data and render critical systems inoperable. Operational errors or natural threats can also negatively impact the operational systems used to deliver critical services.

---

[8] NIST, "Message to Senior Executives on the Cybersecurity Framework," *www.nist.gov/itl/upload/discussion-draft_executive-overview-082813.pdf*

A Key Tool: The Industry-led Cybersecurity Framework

Due to these threats, impacts and risk to our nation's economic and national security, the President issued Executive Order 13636, "Improving Critical Infrastructure Cybersecurity" on February 12, 2013. The Executive Order calls for the development of a voluntary risk-based cybersecurity Framework that is "prioritized, flexible, repeatable, performance-based, and cost-effective", and is developed and implemented in a partnership with owners and operators of the nation's critical infrastructure.

The Framework is being developed through an open process, allowing for a robust technical basis that aligns with business interests. By relying on practices developed, managed, and updated by industry, the Framework will evolve with technological advances and will align with business needs.

The Framework provides a uniform guide for developing robust cybersecurity programs for organizations. This includes industry-driven standards, best practices and implementation measures to manage cybersecurity risks to information technology and operational technology.

The Framework provides a common structure for managing cybersecurity risk, and will help you identify and understand your organization's dependencies with its business partners, vendors, and suppliers. In doing so, it will allow you to coordinate cybersecurity risk within your industry and sector for the delivery of critical infrastructure services.

Unique missions, threats, vulnerabilities, and risk tolerances may require different risk management strategies. One organization's decisions on how to manage cybersecurity risk may differ from another. The Framework is intended to help each organization manage cybersecurity risks while maintaining flexibility and the ability to meet business needs. As a result, the Framework is not designed to replace existing processes. If an organization does not have an existing risk management process for cybersecurity, the Framework provides the tools to build one. By implementing the Framework, an organization can take steps to improve the resilience of its services while protecting data and intellectual property. This methodology is designed to instill trust from the sector and partners and protects the organization's brand and reputation.

Using the Framework

The Framework places cybersecurity activities into five functions: identify, protect, detect, respond, and recover. Organizations should implement capabilities in each of these areas.

Implementing the Framework will help you align and communicate your cybersecurity risk posture with your partners and help communicate expectations for managing cybersecurity risk consistent with your business needs. As the Framework is implemented throughout critical infrastructure, lessons learned and improvements will be integrated, to ensure it is a dynamic and relevant framework. The repeated cybersecurity intrusions into the nation's critical infrastructure have demonstrated the need for a stronger approach to manage cybersecurity. Every organization involved in critical infrastructure services is invited to actively participate in the development, validation, and implementation of CSF.

Page intentionally left blank

Appendix D: Action Planning

To achieve the desired outcomes as described in the CSF and to attain the stakeholder goals identified in implementation Step 1, a comprehensive action plan is necessary. As part of the planning process, implementers should determine the appropriate authorities who will review, approve and track the activities and actions described. It is important that business/mission drivers inform and support these actions.

By linking the actions listed to the enterprise and technical goals (as described in the COBIT 5 goals cascade and as documented as part of implementation Step 1), actions will be assessable and prioritized to achieve the necessary value for the organization. These priorities and the associated actions, may be reviewed and adjusted through periodic checkpoint meetings such as quarterly briefings, program management reviews and security training exercises. A list of action plan data points is shown in **figure D.1**.

Specific considerations for action planning may include the following:
• Are there sector-specific action plan processes?
• Who is responsible for defining actions within the plan?
• How often will action plans be reviewed and updated? By whom?
• What specific governance and management processes apply to your industry to help stay on track?
• What are the advantages to achieving a higher/lower tier?
• What are the disadvantages to achieving a higher/lower tier?
• What regulatory guidance is available to help select the appropriate tier for my organization?
• What agencies, groups, or consortia exist to support organizational compliance and security programs?
• How is feedback captured and disseminated throughout the organization?

Figure D.1—Action Plan Data Points	
Action Plan Detail	**Description**
Action Identifier	Unique identifier assigned to a specific action
Priority	Organizationally defined priority for completing the action (e.g., High, Medium, Low or 1 through 6)
Assumptions/Constraints	Organizationally defined factors that may impact the ability to complete the action
Rationale	Identifies the rationale used to define the action. Links to Profile(s), or regulatory requirements, should be included when available.
Specific action	The discrete, outcome-based, action to be completed
Resources required	The organizational resources required to complete the action
Schedule/Milestones	Key milestones or schedules assigned to the specific action
Status	A stop light indicator (e.g., Green, Amber, Red), or current organizational-approved status indicator, to signify the status of the action and identification of issues that may cause a scheduled milestone to be missed
Prerequisites/dependencies	Identifies other actions or organizational factors that must be completed prior to this action being complete
Action assignee	Point of contact assigned the responsibility for tracking and ensuring that the action is completed
Stakeholder roles	Internal and external organizational stakeholder of the action

Appendix E: Considerations for Critical Infrastructure Sectors

The CSF was developed as directed by EO 13636, in direct support of the critical infrastructure community. For enterprises that are identified with one of the sixteen critical infrastructure sectors listed in **figure 2**, or enterprises that support entities in those sectors, the following considerations may be helpful for implementing the CSF in that context.

Role Identification
From the chairman of the board" to the nuclear reactor operator, roles vary widely among critical infrastructure providers. The CSF generally classifies these roles into three categories as described in chapter 2. The reader is encouraged to determine the applicable titles of each role and refer specifically to those titles in planning/operations/monitoring documents. Doing so will aid in the education and implementation of cybersecurity activities without confusion about disparate role identification.

Implementation Scope
The applicable scope for CSF implementation will vary with each enterprise. Some entities may take an exploratory approach and apply CSF to a subentity to gain experience, while others may apply it to the entire enterprise at once. Such decisions are typically based on organizational business needs and budgets.

The reader should determine whether any legal and/or regulatory drivers will affect that scope. For example, the Health Insurance Portability and Accountability Act (HIPAA) describes specific objectives for "Meaningful Use" of certified electronic health record technology. Jurisdictional considerations may also impact the scope decisions—legal considerations in one country may be quite different from those in another portion of the world. These external drivers may influence the goals considered and the actions taken to improve cybersecurity.

Risk Considerations
Determination of the enterprise risk architecture is an important element of implementation Step 1 because many of the subsequent activities support maintaining a balance between realizing benefits and optimizing risk levels and resource use. Many critical information sectors are subject to external drivers that impact those risk decisions. The financial sector, for example, has many factors that influence acceptable risk considerations. Documentation of these considerations and factors during Step 1 will support subsequent steps and will ensure that these important stakeholder goals are attained and tracked in accordance with regulatory management and reporting requirements.

Quality Management

Quality management overlays closely with effective cybersecurity practices. COBIT 5 process APO11 *Manage quality* describes the use and maintenance of a Quality Management System (QMS). Management practice APO11.01 states, "Establish and maintain a QMS that provides a standard, formal and continuous approach to quality management for information, enabling technology and business processes that are aligned with business requirements and enterprise quality management." Applying the APO11 management practices helps the organization define and manage quality standards, practices, and procedures in accord with the prioritization and risk decisions agreed on in the CSF Implementation steps described earlier in this document. Focusing quality management on customers and the stakeholder goals (as established in Phases 1 and 2), and integrating those quality management processes as part of the action plan will help ensure alignment with mission needs. Performing quality monitoring, control and reviews helps ensure that organizational processes and technology are delivering value to the business, continuous improvement and transparency for stakeholders.

Critical infrastructure providers may have additional QMS requirements for enterprise systems. The relevant goals for management of such a QMS should be considered when developing Profiles and determining actions. Such readers may be guided by standards in the ISO 9000 family, including:
• ISO 9001:2008—Sets out the requirements of a QMS
• ISO 9000:2005—Covers the basic concepts and language
• ISO 9004:2009—Focuses on how to make a QMS more efficient and effective
• ISO 19011:2011—Sets out guidance on internal and external audits of QMS

Threat and Vulnerability Information

Members of the critical infrastructure community are particular targets of cybersecurity threats, often through innovative attack vectors. US users are especially encouraged to work with applicable groups such as Information Sharing and Analysis Centers (ISACs) and the Department of Homeland Security, including the US Computer Emergency Readiness Team (CERT). InfraGard, a partnership between the Federal Bureau of Investigation (FBI) and the private sector, is also helpful. It is an association of people who represent businesses, academic institutions, state and local law enforcement agencies, and other participants dedicated to sharing information and intelligence to prevent hostile acts.

The National Council of ISACs (NCI) may be helpful in identifying ways to assist in enterprise threat and vulnerability understanding. NCI exists to advance the physical and cybersecurity of the critical infrastructures of North America by establishing and maintaining a framework for valuable interaction between and among the ISACs and with government.

The Industrial Control System ISAC (ICS-ISAC) established a project known as the Situational Awareness Reference Architecture (SARA). SARA's objective is to compile and publish an applied guide to the processes, practices, standards and technologies which facilities and others can use to establish situational awareness.

Enterprises should determine the conditions under which a vulnerability may be addressed. For example, some critical systems may not be able to be shut down to support an important patch, so mitigating controls should be identified to ensure appropriate means to achieve enterprise goals for both availability and security. These considerations apply to all people, processes and technology (as described in chapter 1) that enable business functions.

Automated Indicator Sharing

The *NIST Roadmap for Improving Critical Infrastructure Cybersecurity*[9] recommends the use of automated sharing of indicator information to provide organizations with timely, actionable information that they can use to detect and respond to cybersecurity events as they are occurring. Recent intrusions have indicated that adversaries attack multiple sector participants at once, such as recent denial-of-service attacks against many members of the financial sector.

NIST recommends that organizations "use a combination of standard and proprietary mechanisms to exchange indicators that can be used to bolster defenses and to support early detection of future attack attempts. These mechanisms have differing strengths and weaknesses and often require organizations to maintain specific process, personnel, and technical capabilities." CSF implementers are encouraged to work with NIST and sector leadership to adopt and improve practical approaches to achieve automated indicator sharing.

Supply Chain Risk Management

Similarly, NIST promotes increased adoption of standards for supply chain risk management. NIST says that the "adoption of supply chain risk management standards, practices and guidelines requires greater awareness and understanding of the risk associated with the time-sensitive interdependencies throughout the supply chain, including in and between critical infrastructure sectors/subsectors. This understanding is vital to enable organizations to assess their risk, prioritize, and allow for timely mitigation."

CSF implementers are encouraged to include supply chain risk as a subset of the broad risk assessment and risk management activities. More information about supply chain risk management is available from NIST's Computer Security Division.

---

[9] NIST, *NIST Roadmap for Improving Critical Infrastructure Cybersecurity*, USA, 2014, *www.nist.gov/cyberframework/upload/roadmap-021214.pdf*

Current and Target Profiles

During numerous CSF development workshops, NIST pointed out the potential that leadership of individual sectors (e.g., sector supporting agencies, sector councils, participating companies) would provide specific guidance on creation and maintenance of Current and Target Profiles. Such guidance might include: mapping from the CSF Core to compliance frameworks, criteria for determining the thresholds described in **figure 17** or recommendations regarding Core Subcategories.

Framework Next Steps

In announcing the launch of the CSF, the Special Assistant to the US President and the US Cybersecurity Coordinator, Michael Daniel, made three requests that are especially significant for US critical infrastructure community:

• "We need you to kick the tires. We need organizations to begin using the Framework and see how well it can work for different sizes and types of organizations."

• "We need your feedback to make the Framework better. We need you to share your experience with us on how using the Framework worked—or didn't work—for your organization. Feedback is essential to improving the Framework and making it better in future versions."

• "In short, we need your continued engagement. The Framework is intended to be a living document. We need your collective experience and knowledge to make it better over time."

ISACA encourages all who implement this initial version of the Cybersecurity Framework to help improve its value, to provide feedback to the CSF community and help this framework achieve its goal of improving cybersecurity risk management. Through ISACA's leadership and the new Cybersecurity Nexus (CSX), ISACA membership can be particularly helpful to achieve that goal and safeguard enterprises around the globe.